D1645687

THE CALI
CARTEL
BEYOND NARCOS

WAR ON DRUGS BOOK 4

SHAUN ATTWOOD

For Aunt Lily and the kids

ACKNOWLEDGEMENTS

A big thank you to Emma Bagnell,
Penny Kimber (proofreading),
Jane Dixon-Smith (typesetting and cover formatting)

This book was written in British English, hence USA readers may notice some spelling differences with American English.

GET A FREE BOOK

Sign Up For My Newsletter:

http://shaunattwood.com/newsletter-subscribe/

SHAUN'S BOOKS

English Shaun Trilogy
Party Time
Hard Time
Prison Time

War on Drugs Series
Pablo Escobar: Beyond Narcos
American Made: Who Killed Barry Seal? Pablo Escobar or George HW Bush
The Cali Cartel: Beyond Narcos
We Are Being Lied To: The War on Drugs (Expected 2018)

Un-Making a Murderer: The Framing of Steven Avery and Brendan Dassey

Life Lessons

Two Tonys (Expected 2019)
T-Bone (Expected 2022)

SOCIAL-MEDIA LINKS

Email: attwood.shaun@hotmail.co.uk
Blog: Jon's Jail Journal
Website: shaunattwood.com
Twitter: @shaunattwood
YouTube: Shaun Attwood
LinkedIn: Shaun Attwood
Goodreads: Shaun Attwood
Facebook: Shaun Attwood, Jon's Jail Journal, T-Bone
Appreciation Society

I welcome feedback on any of my books.
Thank you for the Amazon and Goodreads reviews!

CONTENTS

CHAPTER 1
A SOCCER GAME

On September 25, 1990, Pacho Herrera – the youngest of the four Cali Cartel godfathers – was playing soccer with his brother and bodyguards at a personal ranch called the Coconuts, on a remote piece of land surrounded by sugarcane fields. Holding cans of beer and soda, about fifty men were sitting on the grass and rows of wooden benches cheering at the players in sports uniforms on a pitch illuminated better than any stadium in Colombia. Directing one of the teams was a former pro footballer, which added to the excitement. The Tuesday-evening game had attracted an increasing number of spectators, including workers from the neighbouring farms such as cane cutters, who relished cooling off. Despite the threat from the rival Medellín Cartel, Pacho's security was lax.

In the preceding days, twenty assassins – sent by Pablo Escobar – had drifted into the area. Travelling by bus, either alone or in small units, they had arrived unnoticed. Mostly in their late teens, they had rendezvoused at a farmhouse near the village of Santander.

Local people tended to report the arrival of strangers to the Cali Cartel, which paid taxi drivers and others to be its eyes and ears. Anyone protecting outsiders ran the risk of torture, death and the massacre of their families. But Pablo had outsmarted the Cali Cartel by sending young unarmed men covertly and renting an assembly point from a farmer known to keep his mouth shut for the right price.

Deliveries arrived at the farmhouse: a variety of military uniforms, two trucks and AR-15 automatic rifles capable of spraying a crowd with bullets in a matter of seconds. On the night of the game, Pablo's men put on the uniforms and grabbed the guns. They got into two trucks with sky-blue cabins. Brown canvas over the rear of the trucks concealed them. They drove for about twenty minutes.

Clean shaven and in excellent shape, Pacho was focused on the game when the first truck parked at around 7 pm. The play continued as armed men in uniforms emerged from the darkness. As the local authorities were in the pocket of the Cali Cartel, everyone assumed that the soldiers had stopped by on a friendly basis. No one noticed the hodgepodge of uniforms and that the soldiers were mostly wearing sneakers not boots. As the soccer players were unarmed, the assassins initially aimed their guns at those in charge of surveillance and the rows of spectators.

Bam-bam-bam-bam-bam-bam...

The AR-15s fired so fast that the shots were impossible to count. The players stopped chasing the ball. Their gaze swung to the slaughter of the spectators, some of whom flopped down in pools of blood. Those unharmed stampeded away as the guns cut down some of the players. A lady in the kitchen heard the shots and abandoned the food that she had been preparing.

Pacho, his brother and others sprinted over the field into the darkness. When they felt they had gone a safe distance, they hid in the thick of the crops. Eventually, the shots ended, indicating that the assassins had fled. Warily, Pacho and the survivors returned to the Coconuts. Yelling in Spanish, they rushed to almost twenty corpses of relatives and friends. Others were leaking blood, writhing, moaning and begging for help. With fire in his eyes, Pacho pledged revenge against Pablo.

In green military garb, police with rifles arrived, rushed around and questioned the survivors, who were dazed, injured or angry. Corpses were loaded onto a truck and transported to the morgue.

Eager to earn extra money from the Cali Cartel, the police combed the area. Two young men were discovered on a remote road. The police grew suspicious after the men claimed that they had been staying with friends and were trying to get a bus to

Medellín, yet were walking in the wrong direction. In jail, interrogated by a representative of the Cali Cartel, they detailed the entire plot, including the farmhouse they had stayed at.

At the farm, the police found uniforms, weapons and vehicles. The farmer's siblings claimed that their brother had vanished without telling them anything. A week later, two of the farmer's brothers and a sister were found shot in the head. Pacho ordered the execution of the two hit men in the local jail, which prisoners handled with homemade knives. He dispatched his own assassins after the farmer, who remained elusive.

It took two and a half years for the cartel to catch the farmer. A helicopter transported him to a ranch belonging to Pacho. The cartel men studied the man with a bruised face as he sat at a table in a stable, holding a cigarette. They knew his fate.

The two senior godfathers arrived last. Everyone hushed. Gilberto and Miguel Rodríguez Orejuela were short stocky brothers who sported thin beards or goatees. The elder, Gilberto, was a charmer who used eloquent words even though he had not finished high school. When it came to speaking, Miguel was a Spartan who had such a sour disposition that he had earned the nickname Lemon. Displaying little emotion, the dark-eyed godfathers studied the farmer.

With an air of command, Gilberto told the captive that he was in big trouble. The farmer stared at the ground, nonchalant. Gilberto said that the farmer was delusional to have thought that he could have got away with it, and that the farmer must have believed that he was so smart and they were so stupid. Remaining silent, the farmer smoked.

"Why did you help Pablo?"

In a calm way that startled his captors, the farmer looked at Gilberto and admitted that he had made a mistake. He had taken money to accommodate visitors, who had left him in the dark about their intentions. Gilberto asked if the farmer knew what was going to happen to him. The farmer gazed down.

The godfathers departed except for Pacho, who had a fierce

look in his eyes. Cartel men removed the farmer's boots and shirt. He flailed as his legs were tied to the back of a truck and his arms attached to another. Men spat on him and kicked him. After the farmer was securely attached to both vehicles, their engines revved and they slowly moved away from each other. His arms and legs stretched to an abnormal length and eventually popped out of their sockets. The farmer urinated and released a primal animal-like scream. For half an hour, what remained of him was reattached to the trucks, which moved slightly and slowly to torture him for as long as possible until he stopped breathing.

CHAPTER 2
THE GODFATHERS

The two most powerful Cali Cartel godfathers were Gilberto and his younger brother Miguel. Gilberto was known as the Chess Player due to his knack for using cold calculation to outsmart the authorities and his rivals. Charismatic and well-mannered, Gilberto sported a tidy beard. Typically, he dressed in business attire or expensive casual clothes. Despite the horror of what had happened at the farmhouse, he preferred to use bribery over violence to keep the cocaine empire running smoothly. While Pablo Escobar waged war with the government of Colombia, the Cali Cartel had such good relations with politicians that the authorities only went through the motions of pursuing the Cali godfathers. Through bribery, the gentlemen from Cali secured friends at all levels of society, ranging from the police and judges, right up to the president.

Out of the two brothers, Gilberto was considered to be more cerebral. His refined tastes included a passion for Colombian poetry. Both brothers loved soccer so much that they invested in teams and built pitches. While Gilberto was responsible for the long-term strategy of the cartel, Miguel was a micro-manager who enjoyed being in charge of the day-to-day operations. Miguel used phones and fax machines to collect information and to communicate instructions to employees. He was renowned for wanting to know every little detail. Before the war with the Medellín Cartel, the Orejuela brothers had gained the respect of traffickers nationwide, who used the honorific Don when addressing them. Cartel employees viewed Gilberto as a kindly uncle, whereas they were terrified of Miguel.

Gilberto was born on January 30, 1939, near Mariquita,

Tolima, a picturesque town close to the Magdalena River, just over ninety miles northwest of Bogotá. Miguel was born there on August 15, 1943. Growing up, they lived in the poor Balthazar barrio of Cali. In a *Time Magazine* article titled "A Day with the Chess Player," Gilberto said:

"I was born between the towns of Mariquita and Honda Tolima. My father was a painter and a draftsman, and my mother was a housewife. We were three brothers and three sisters. When I was 15, I started working as a clerk in a drugstore in Cali. By the time I was 20, I was the manager, and at 25, 10 years after entering the business, I quit in order to start my own drugstore."

Miguel claimed to have a law degree, but a US government witness insisted that Miguel had bought the degree by donating a library to the university and lavishing the dean with gifts.

Despite the air of civility that they cultivated in public, the two brothers rose up in the crime world through kidnapping – just like Pablo Escobar – and building dangerous reputations. They were arrested for counterfeiting, but the judge let the statute of limitations on their trial lapse because of the death threats she had received. Masters of avoiding detection, they operated under numerous fake names, backed up by counterfeit passports and official documents.

With eight children each, the brothers had such large families that during the war with Pablo they had a permanent staff of 150 people protecting them. Gilberto had three wives and Miguel had four. Miguel's children ranged in age from three-year-old Andrea to William, a law student in his mid-20s. Gilberto's children were slightly older. Their children were schooled overseas. Some ended up in Harvard and Stanford Universities. Gilberto's eldest son was arrested for drugs and incarcerated in a Cali jail. Gilberto was so distressed that he went to the jail, pulled out a belt and whipped his son to teach him a lesson to avoid drugs.

In later years, Gilberto told *Time Magazine* that his children had all grown up to be professionals and one was a student. After earning degrees at European and American universities, they had been employed by Gilberto's businesses. The brothers also had their mother, three sisters and a younger brother whom they had nicknamed Good For Nothing.

Having four wives brought its own set of problems for Miguel. They generally remained in their own homes, but sometimes they stayed at his main house. When a wife was scheduled to visit, Miguel's housekeeper was under strict instructions to hide any evidence of the previous wifely visits. The technique she used involved photographing the bedroom immediately after a wife had departed. By the time the same wife returned, the house-keeper had used the photograph to restore the bedroom to its original order. A crisis arose when Miguel's second wife, Ampara, the mother of three of his children, found a pair of fluffy pink slippers under the bed that belonged to Miguel's fourth wife, Marta, an ex-beauty queen and the mother of his three-year-old. The slippers had eluded the photograph taken when Marta had departed. After the incident, the housekeeper had to take extra precautions to prevent any further mishaps.

Miguel's third wife, Fabiola, was a witch who manipulated energy to heal and protect people. Her house was adorned with red ribbons, crystal balls, amulets and charms purported to possess occult powers. She burned incense and cultivated aloe plants. She kept raw eggs floating in glasses hidden around the house.

Even with four wives, Miguel still engaged in new romances, including the widow of one of the cartel's victims. A Cali lieu-tenant, Claudio Endo, had ordered the assassination of some people who owed him money. Unfortunately, one of his victims was close to hit men who worked for the Cali godfathers Pacho and Chepe. The hit men lobbied for vengeance, and the godfa-thers authorised Endo's murder. By listening to Endo's phone, the cartel tracked him to a ranch where he was spending time with his family. Hit men arrived in cars and launched an assault. They annihilated Endo's bodyguards and smashed down the front door. Leaving his wife and daughter in the living room, Endo dashed into a bathroom at the back of the house, where he was trapped.

After surrounding him, the hit men shot him over 100 times. According to Ron Chepesiuk in *The Bullet or the Bribe*, Miguel satisfied his crush on Endo's wife by dating her over half a year after her husband's funeral.

In their thirties, the brothers founded the Cali Cartel in the 1970s with the third godfather, Jose Santacruz Londono. Known as Chepe, Londono was born on October 1, 1943 in Cali, the most populous city in southwest Colombia. All three godfathers were friends at high school. In the 1970s, Chepe was arrested twice, once for a weapons violation in America. His kidnapping résumé included a university student and an industrialist. He parlayed money from kidnapping into a fleet of taxis. Upon suspecting that his wife was going to leave Colombia with his children and settle in Miami, Chepe had her killed because he thought he would never see his kids again. An informant told the DEA that Chepe's wife was always yelling and screaming and complaining, and he was not the type who would put up with that forever. A journalist out of New York who had criticised Chepe was assassinated.

After the rejection of his application for Club Colombia – exclusively for businessmen and industrialists – Chepe did not order the disappearance of the decision-makers. After he had calmed down, he decided to build his own exclusive club based on the design of Club Colombia on a hillside in a luxurious neighbourhood. He also commissioned a country club to be built with statues of heroes, three large white crosses and a bridge.

The earliest documented kidnappings occurred when the three godfathers were teenagers. A kidnapped fisherman resulted in Gilberto spending a day in jail. In the late 1960s, they joined a gang that kidnapped two Swiss citizens: a student and a diplomat. Aged twenty-eight and running a gang of seven kidnappers, Gilberto negotiated a ransom of 12 million pesos, which was almost $1 million at the time. The three godfathers invested that money first into marijuana and then into the far more profitable cocaine business.

In the 1970s, Chepe started to build cocaine distribution throughout America. Gilberto and Miguel concentrated on processing the raw material in labs in Peru and Colombia. Individual parts of the business were set up as self-contained cells, so that if the authorities discovered them, the workers genuinely couldn't provide any information about the rest of the self-contained parts of the Cali Cartel. Miguel took reports from the people in charge of the individual parts such as the regional bosses of Southern Florida and New York. Information concerning finances, security, drug shipments and the police was submitted to Miguel.

Pacho was the fourth godfather to join the executive board. Out of all of the Cali godfathers, Pacho kept the lowest profile. He rarely allowed interviews. Due to his strong business performance, his homosexuality was accepted by the godfathers.

Pacho grew up in Palmira, a town less than an hour's drive east of Cali. In high school, he studied technical maintenance. He used his education to get a job in America, where he became a jeweller and a precious metals broker until he began selling cocaine. In 1975 and later in 1978, he was arrested on cocaine distribution charges in New York.

After getting released from US prison in 1983, Pacho went to Cali to negotiate with the godfathers for supply and distribution rights in New York, where he started to build his empire. As law enforcement increasingly policed the Florida border, Pacho used his contacts to shift the smuggling routes to Mexico, which was extremely lucrative for the cartel. According to the DEA, Pacho ran one of the "most sophisticated and profitable money laundering operations."

Pacho dealt harshly with his enemies. Those suspected of betraying him were invited to one of his large ranches for a feast. After they had eaten, he would lead them to a room, put bags over their heads and torture them into confessing. Their corpses ended up in the Cauca River. Another preferred method of enemy disposal involved flying them to Cali, killing them and sending lookalikes back on return flights. That way the authorities and the victims' family members were led to believe that the victims had disappeared at the other end of the journey.

The Cali and Medellín cartels had different organisational

structures. The Medellín was an alliance between independent operators, whereas Cali was run by a four-man executive board. Below the board were accountants, engineers and lawyers, and then the workforce. The executives, some of whom had law degrees, considered themselves more sophisticated than the rustic men from Medellín. They were known as the gentlemen of trafficking, whereas the Medellín Cartel was regarded as thuggish. The head of the New York DEA told journalists, "Cali gangs will kill you if they have to, but they prefer to use a lawyer."

Whereas members of the Medellín Cartel were sometimes at odds, the Cali godfathers never had a major disagreement. Pablo tended to impose his will upon others, but the men from Cali shared equal votes for key decisions. When they went to war with Pablo, they stuck together even more tightly.

If you look at a map of Central and South America, the Cali Cartel's cocaine production started in the south with the growth of the leaves in Bolivia and Peru. To get the finished product north to America, the leaves were transported up to Colombia and processed into cocaine. Colombia was ideal for labs due to its size: more than four times bigger than the UK; almost twice the size of Texas or France. In the dense jungles and forests, illegal activity was easily disguised from the poorly funded and ill-equipped authorities. With Colombia being at the top of South America, the cocaine continued northbound through Central America, stopping at friendly transshipment points and finally crossing America's southern border.

Cali is the capital city of the Cauca Valley, an area of Colombia's western side, which faces the Pacific Ocean. It's a place where tourists enjoy salsa music, panoramic mountain views, historic church buildings and constant tropical warmth because it's so near to the Equator. This picturesque agricultural region is an industrial and commercial centre for coffee, cotton, sugarcane and soybeans, which are shipped through the city. Tyres, tobacco products, textiles, paper, chemicals and building materials are manufactured there. The town centre is noisy with traffic and bars playing Spanish songs. On the streets, poor people peddle their wares, including candy, clothes, shoes and little gold trinkets of Inca gods and frogs.

In the 1980s, Cali's population was over 1 million. The godfathers maintained control by using their influence over the telephone company. Through bribery, cartel technicians and engineers could listen to any calls. The cartel had thousands of taxi drivers on its payroll. Clustered at the airport, they reported the arrival of anyone who aroused their suspicion, especially Americans in case they were working for the DEA.

The godfathers split Cali into fiefdoms. Gilberto and Miguel controlled Cali's centre, an area around the Intercontinental Hotel in downtown Cali, and Ciudad Jardin in the southernmost part of Cali, home to the wealthiest residents. Chepe had the southern region of Cali. Pacho's cities included Palmira and Yumbo, north of Cali, and Jamundi, a city 50 miles south of Cali.

The godfathers had luxury properties in each area on pieces of land protected by walls. Adjacent to their dwellings were swimming pools, tennis courts, bowling alleys, cockfighting arenas, horse stables, dance clubs, private beaches and soccer pitches. To keep a low profile when outside their properties they drove Mazdas. The luxury cars they owned were loaned out to politicians and prominent people.

The media reported a house owned by Miguel as including four bedrooms, seven living rooms, endless expensive furniture, a lion skin rug, a stuffed lion, hundreds of porcelain figurines that cost up to $3,000 each, and a glass bead curtain hanging from a second-floor ceiling above an indoor reflecting pool. At each end of the house were spiral staircases: one led to a sky-lit gym; the other to a bar with an underwater view of an outdoor pool.

To control the local population, the cartel bribed key people in politics, law enforcement and business. They threw parties for hundreds of officials. Gilberto's bank gave shareholdings to local leaders, some of whom ended up on the bank's board of directors, making them eligible for preferential loans and overdrafts.

The godfathers' grip on the police was so strong that when a love rival shot his competitor dead at a urinal during a salsa concert financed by the godfathers, the homicide detectives who arrived to investigate the crime scene were instructed to wait outside so as not to upset the gentlemen from Cali or to disrupt the concert. After six hours, the detectives were allowed inside. All of the witnesses were long gone and no one dared to provide any information. As the hit was unsanctioned, the godfathers summoned the murderer to appear before them. Miguel said that the godfathers didn't care why the man had been killed. They felt disrespected; they had a reputation to uphold in Cali. The man begged for his life, which was spared.

In the media, they credited their legitimate business interests for generating their wealth. If there were negative reports about them, Gilberto would often pick up the phone and chastise the journalists. During the war with Pablo, they portrayed themselves as businessmen victims of a narco-terrorist.

Potential cartel employees had to fill out applications. They hired the most talented people, including accountants, economists and financial advisers. New employees were faxed the rules, which included living modestly and avoiding attracting attention. Stash-house operators were instructed to keep the normal hours of a working person by leaving in the morning and returning at night.

Out of the hundreds of traffickers in Colombia, the disciplined application of business techniques enabled the Cali Cartel to forge ahead. In the 1970s and early 80s, the traffickers generally got along with the exception of the odd minor dispute.

By the early 1980s, the Cali and Medellín traffickers had amassed fortunes that attracted predators. In July 1981, Pablo Escobar obtained a recording of the M-19 guerrillas, who were devising a plan to kidnap a trafficker. Pablo arranged a meeting with four of the guerrillas, whose backgrounds and secret locations he had investigated thoroughly. Confronted with eighty armed men working for Pablo, one of the guerrillas held up a grenade with its safety pin removed as a strategy to protect himself. Pablo revealed what he knew about them, including the locations of their safe houses and the names of fourteen guerrillas in the Medellín chapter. He said that he knew their plans before they had even been implemented, and it was best that neither side messed with the other. Intimidated by his knowledge and show of force, the guerrillas agreed not to kidnap traffickers. Pablo sent them on their way with a contribution of over $10,000.

There was lots of infighting among the guerrilla leadership. Some wanted negotiations with the government, whereas others wanted war. By November 1981, their truce with Pablo fell apart. According to Rodney Stich in *Drugging America,* the CIA paid the M-19 $3 million – $2 million in weapons and $1 million in cash – to abduct a senior Medellín cartel member and the sister of the Ochoa faction of the Medellín Cartel. The senior member of the cartel managed to escape by bailing out of a moving car, but he was shot and injured as he fled. The Ochoa sister was successfully kidnapped and millions were demanded for her return.

Pablo and the most powerful trafficking families held a meeting to formulate a plan to deter the M-19 from any further kidnappings of their family members and associates. A few hundred senior traffickers from across Colombia attended. The Medellín and Cali Cartels were united. If the M-19 received millions in return for the Ochoa sister, it would set a precedent and all of their family members would be at risk. The traffickers decided to form an army called Death to Kidnappers. The Castaño brothers – who later on allied with the CIA and the Cali Cartel against Pablo – played leading roles in Death to Kidnappers because their father had been killed by guerrillas. Guerrillas were captured and tortured for information. Dozens were slaughtered. The M-19 had underestimated the traffickers, who did more damage to them in a brief period than the Colombian army had in years. Following a meeting in Panama, which included Pablo, the Ochoas and the M-19, the guerrillas apologised and released the hostage.

The threat from the kidnappers strengthened relations among the traffickers across Colombia. They started to pool their resources and work collaboratively on smuggling drugs into America, where demand was so high that there was plenty of room for all of them to coexist without engaging in petty wars.

There was little heat from the US government yet because heroin and marijuana were the priority of the DEA. The main aim of US foreign policy was preventing the spread of Communism. The CIA didn't want cocaine production falling into the hands of Communists in Central and South America. Fighting left-wing guerrillas and contributing to the anti-Communism crusade earned the traffickers CIA protection and endless supplies of American weapons. In the early years, the Cali Cartel and Pablo were working with the CIA, as Pablo's son has stated in his second book.

One of Pablo's biggest mistakes was to run for political office. He wasn't the first trafficker in South America to attempt to control a country by direct involvement in politics. Just a few years earlier in Bolivia in 1980, cocaine traffickers had orchestrated a coup with the help of the Argentine intelligence services, the CIA and the Nazi Klaus Barbie a.k.a. the Butcher of Lyon. The coup had increased the production of cocaine flowing from Bolivia through Colombia to America – a trend that the Colombian cartels had capitalised on.

But Pablo's foray into politics drew the attention of the media and the power-hungry Vice President George HW Bush to Pablo's cocaine business. President Nixon had earned more votes by railing against drugs – a strategy which had not gone unnoticed by Bush. The gentlemen of Cali wisely preferred to take a backseat to the limelight, and not be targeted by politicians. Making money covertly was their priority.

Planes transported millions of dollars to Colombia for both cartels. Although Pablo invested in numerous construction projects such as his ranch estate Hacienda Nápoles, which cost almost $100 million and hosted the largest zoo in Colombia, he was also renowned for burying money. While he lost millions of dollars due to water damage and rats eating the cash, the Cali Cartel avoided that by immediately investing it into business projects, which included drugstores, banks, car dealerships, radio stations, shipping and football teams. Their property investments caused a real estate and construction boom in Cali, which served to further endear them to the locals. The Cali Cartel encouraged people to invest in cocaine shipments. The astronomical returns bought more peace.

In 1984, Gilberto was in Spain with Jorge Ochoa, one of the leaders of the Medellín Cartel. With the authorities launching raids on traffickers in Colombia, the two godfathers had escaped the heat by settling into an 8,000-square-foot mansion, complete with a swimming pool, tennis courts, a disco and four Mercedes-Benz.

The trip to Spain was no holiday. The godfathers were eager to expand their illegal enterprise into Europe because the street price of cocaine in America had dropped due to oversupply. European street prices were up to four times higher. They chose the border area with Portugal as a potential headquarters. To learn about the best routes and storage methods, they consulted tobacco smugglers from Galicia. They decided on transporting the cocaine by ship and using smaller boats to bring the cocaine onto the land. The cash would be laundered through a dizzyingly complex number of steps, which included bank accounts in Spain, Panama and real estate investments. Ochoa dispatched a lieutenant to Berlin, Amsterdam and London to set up distribution networks using Colombian communities. A British pilot married to an Ochoa cousin personally flew hundreds of kilos to America, and shipped them to the UK, sparking a cocaine surge that saw UK seizures double. Gangsters in Liverpool facilitated the importation of Colombian cocaine through its shipping port. In Europe, confiscated cocaine increased from 900 kilos in 1985 to thirteen tonnes by 1990.

After an informant snitched on Gilberto and Jorge Ochoa, the

Spanish police set up surveillance. They watched the godfathers living luxuriously, frequenting restaurants and concerts. They learned that Ochoa's wife was depositing hundreds of thousands of dollars in local banks, which they concluded was hot money.

The Spanish authorities notified the DEA, who told Washington: "Intelligence… has indicated that suspected Colombian trafficking group intends to create investment company with unlimited funding and is in the process of purchasing several extremely expensive residences, indicating intent to remain in Spain."

For almost three months, the Spanish authorities monitored the godfathers. After Ochoa asked about buying 10,000 acres in southern Spain, the police feared that he was about to set up a global cocaine hub.

On November 15, 1984, the two godfathers and their wives were arrested. Attempting to capitalise on the windfall, the Americans made overtures to the Spanish in the hope of getting the Colombians extradited. The stage was set for a lengthy legal battle.

In jail for two years, the godfathers employed strategies to avoid extradition to America, where they would never get out of prison. Gilberto transferred the running of the Cali Cartel to his brother, Miguel, and asked Colombia's Ministry of Justice to help him dodge extradition to America. But as the Chess Player had no outstanding warrants in Colombia because he'd shrewdly avoided legal trouble, the Ministry of Justice had no grounds to extradite him to Colombia. A charge of bull smuggling was invented, and cartel lawyers made a fuss about imperialistic America interfering in the legal systems of sovereign nations.

Much to the disappointment of the Americans, Spain extradited the godfathers to Colombia. Ochoa later claimed to have paid $6 million to the Spanish judges. A judge in Cali acquitted Gilberto of the drug smuggling charge. The Cali Cartel paid $1 million to the Colombian Ministry of Justice.

Although the two cartel godfathers had been close enough to

live together in Spain, the relationship between the cartels broke down in the late 1980s. The consequences were deadly.

CHAPTER 3
CARTEL WAR BEGINS

The conflict between the cartels was brewing before its trigger point. Due to constant expansion, the cartels were destined to bump into each other. The Cali Cartel had dominated the New York market, but the Medellín Cartel started to muscle in. Shifting smuggling away from Florida, Cali formed an alliance with the Guadalajara Cartel in Mexico, which incensed Pablo.

An early warning sign of the trouble was the arrest of Jorge Ochoa in November 1986 at a tollgate near Palmira, which is 17 miles east of Cali. With his own surveillance helicopter travelling above him, Ochoa was going to a meeting that Pablo had convened to discuss the formation of a super cartel, which Pablo would lead. Ochoa was accompanied by the girlfriend of one of the Cali Cartel's intermediaries with the Medellín Cartel. The jealous intermediary told the police to watch out for a white Porsche. When the police pulled the car over, the girlfriend Ochoa was having an affair with was on the front seat. Bribery from $10 up to $400,000 offered by Ochoa was refused. He ended up in a maximum-security prison. The US requested his extradition.

With Gilberto in control of the authorities in and around Cali, Ochoa's arrest should never have happened. Even if a mistake had occurred, Gilberto would have been notified immediately and should have rectified the situation. Why would he abandon his partner in crime from Spain?

The Cali godfathers attended the super-cartel meeting. Pablo pitched the economies of scale and the combined economic and political power they would wield. As its leader, Pablo would be vested with the power to authorise every shipment, and he would be paid 30% of each shipment's wholesale value. The Cali godfathers' lack of enthusiasm for his proposal upset Pablo so much that he left the meeting ranting about war.

The cartels started snitching out each other's cocaine shipments to the DEA. In February 1987, the DEA's Miami branch received a letter postmarked from Cali claiming that a ship called *Amazon Sky* was on its way to Saint Petersburg, Florida, with cocaine valued at almost $2 billion. On April 20, agents arrived to inspect the ship's cargo. A broken cedar board roused their suspicion. They drilled into it. After the drill was extracted, it was covered in white powder. Each board contained 1 kilo of cocaine. The DEA estimated that it must have taken up to 1,000 workers to load so much cocaine.

Rather than bust the load, the agents used glue and sandpaper to restore the cedar boards. They put the ship under surveillance. It took four days for all of the cedar boards to be moved to a warehouse complex in Saint Petersburg. The agents filmed the warehouse and listened to its telephone. After two weeks, three men were arrested.

The incident that sparked the full-scale war involved a conflict between Pablo and the Cali godfather Pacho, who at 36 was making billions and gaining considerable power. Two Colombian traffickers in New York had an argument over a woman that turned deadly. Associates of the murdered trafficker turned to Pablo for justice. Upon learning that Pablo's men were after him, the trafficker sought protection from someone he had bonded with in prison as a cellmate: Pacho. After he found out that Pacho had agreed to protect the trafficker, Pablo extended the death penalty to Pacho.

The Cali godfathers decided to protect Pacho. They tried to negotiate with the Medellín Cartel, pointing out that a feud over such a trivial matter would damage them both disproportionately. Gilberto got on the phone with Pablo, who not only refused to change his mind, but ended the conversation with a declaration of war and threatened to kill all of the Cali godfathers.

The Cali Cartel targeted the Monaco Building, where Pablo's

family lived in a 16,000-square-foot two-storey penthouse. Reinforced steel protected the white eight-storey building, which had a swimming pool behind it and palm trees around it. It had a walk-in safe the size of a room, which contained mountains of cash to use for bribes. According to Juan Pablo Escobar in *Pablo Escobar: My Father*, the Escobars ate at a twenty-four-seat dining table in the penthouse to music played by a live violinist. The large linen tablecloths – manufactured by Venetian artisans – had taken up to four years to embroider. The silver dishware had been crafted by Georg Jensen, a Danish silversmith. It included a monogram combining Pablo's and his wife's surnames. Flown from Bogotá to Medellín, fresh flowers were delivered twice a week. Pablo told Maria Victoria that if Aristotle Onassis could send for warm bread in Paris for Jacqueline Kennedy Onassis, then Pablo could at least use a plane to acquire flowers for his wife in Bogotá. Pablo hosted a private tennis tournament at the building. The winner received a car, which wealthy winners donated to a poor family.

In January 1988, the Cali Cartel dispatched one of its top assassins known as Freckles, who looked like the actor Nicolas Cage. Freckles was so loyal to the cartel that he had even murdered his own brother for betraying Miguel. In a car laden with dynamite, Freckles parked under the Monaco Building.

After eating dinner in the Monaco Building on January 12, 1988, Pablo left his family and hid out at a farm ten miles away. Around 5:30 am, the dynamite exploded, waking people up within a two-mile radius. The blast killed two night watchmen, left a crater in the street thirteen feet deep, shattered windows throughout the neighbourhood, broke water mains and cracked the entire face of the building. Within minutes, a Renault arrived to transport Pablo's family to a safe house.

Pablo made a call. "Mom, you'll soon watch some news about a bomb in Monaco. But I just called you, so you'd know nothing happened to me."

By the time Pablo's brother Roberto showed up, Pablo said he already knew who was responsible. Half an hour after the explosion, he'd received a call from the Cali Cartel's Gilberto, who said he'd heard about the bomb and wanted to know if Pablo and his family were OK. Rumours were circulating that the bomb had been planted by DAS agents, but Pablo suspected Gilberto.

Pablo knew that Gilberto had spent time in a Spanish prison with a bomb-maker for the Basque guerrillas. Pablo tracked the bomb-maker down, asked him to train some of his workers and promised him excellent prices on cocaine to sell in Spain. After the bomb-maker agreed, Pablo asked if he'd ever had any experience working in Colombia. The man replied that he'd met someone in jail who'd brought him to Colombia to train some guys to make a bomb to be used against the government. Surrounded by armed bodyguards, Pablo said that the bomb had been used against him. The bomb-maker's face turned white. Pablo told him not to worry and urged him to start to train Pablo's workers.

Gilberto called Pablo, protesting that he hadn't done anything. Pablo told him to stop lying and to get ready to be hit.

A car bomb exploded by Pablo's mother's house. Cut by glass, she was hospitalised. Pablo's pregnant sister had been asleep on the fourth floor. In hospital, she gave birth to a baby that had to live in an incubator for several weeks. Another sister on the fifth floor was treated for shrapnel wounds.

Regarding the Cali Cartel, Pablo told his mother, "If they broke my heart it was because they placed the first bomb."

The Cali Cartel offered a band of killers from Medellín $5 million to kill Pablo, but he hired the killers himself. Pablo ordered the bombing of the drugstores through which Cali laundered lots of its money. The bombs that went off at Drogas la Rebaja killed mostly customers and passers-by. Cali sent seven more killers after Pablo, who sent boxes containing their body parts back to Cali. A bomb exploded half a mile from Miguel's residence, which destroyed three houses. Intended for the Cali godfather, the bomb had gone off prematurely, killing the assassins in charge of it.

The damage to each side shattered any prospect of peace and locked the cartels into a fight to the death.

CHAPTER 4
BRITISH MERCENARIES

Even with the resources of the Colombian government and the Cali Cartel pitted against him, Pablo was proving difficult to kill. The Cali godfathers turned to their head of security for ideas.

Over six-foot tall, Jorge Salcedo towered over most of his peers. The soft-spoken ex-army officer had short dark hair, thick eyebrows, a well-trimmed moustache and a firm gaze. He was a family man, who held degrees in mechanical engineering and industrial economics. Early in his career, he had designed forklifts and other machinery. His father was a retired Colombian army general and a diplomatic figure. Regarding himself as more of an engineer than a soldier, he became proficient in electronic surveillance, which drew him into counterterrorism assignments.

In a previous job for the military financed by the Medellín Cartel's Gacha a.k.a. the Mexican, Jorge had worked with mercenaries based in the UK. Enticed to Colombia on the pretext of fighting Communism, the mercenaries had found themselves embroiled in a turf war over cocaine labs. The mercenaries had been well paid. Their leader, David Tomkins, was enthused about doing more work in Colombia.

With coiffured grey hair, dark brows, narrow features and a tattooed arm, Tomkins was a demolitions expert and soldier of fortune who found solace in the hotspots of the world. His career as a mercenary had started in Africa. In Afghanistan, he fought with the Mujahedeen, in Croatia with warlords, and in Uganda he was involved in a plot to assassinate President Idi Amin. In Angola, a mine exploded on him. He was operated on, but his wounds deteriorated into near gangrene. Back in the UK, he was hospitalised. Two days later, when the nurses came to dress his wounds, they found that he had returned to the battlefield.

As detailed in his book, *Dirty Combat*, Tomkins received a call from Jorge in February 1989. "Are you prepared to come back for another mission?"

"Yes, subject to terms and conditions."

On February 13, Jorge greeted Tomkins at the Bogotá airport. "Your prospective clients," Jorge said, "are a group of businessmen whom Pablo Escobar has sworn to kill. The Medellín Cartel has engaged in a bombing campaign against their business interests. They live in Cali, which is Colombia's third-largest city. More than thirty bombs have exploded in their Drogas La Rebaja chain of 350 stores."

"Why has Pablo Escobar targeted them?" Tomkins pressed Jorge into revealing that the clients were the Cali Cartel. The express purpose of the mission was to kill Pablo Escobar. Although the mission had no official government backing, the authorities had blessed it.

Back in England, Tomkins recruited some colleagues. On February 24, they flew to Colombia. In Cali, they were situated in a five-star apartment with lots of security. They had their own bar, en suite bathrooms and money-counting machines. After they showered, land cruisers transported them to a little town outside Cali called Jamundi, which Pacho controlled. The four godfathers arranged to meet them in a private sports facility with a swimming pool, gym, sauna and running track.

After getting into a complex surrounded by sheet-steel fencing and through security checkpoints, Tomkins and his three colleagues were escorted to the godfathers, who were sat around a table with drinks, wearing tailored shirts, designer trousers, Gucci shoes and watches made by Cartier or Rolex, but of the more modest designs. In a Sergio Tachini sports suit and with designer stubble, Pacho stood out as the youngest. Chepe wore overalls and no socks. A long-sleeved shirt hid his skin condition. As the godfathers spoke in Spanish and the mercenaries in English, Jorge translated. Discussing the operation, the godfathers were relaxed and congenial, as if it were just another day at the office.

Tomkins pulled out a cigarette and scanned the room for ashtrays, but there were none. "Do you mind?" he said to the godfathers.

Miguel shook his head. His face puckered. The godfathers had a strict policy of no substances being used during work time. Jorge explained that Miguel was allergic to smoke.

At lunchtime, the front gates allowed in a three-tonne open-back truck with over a dozen policemen. Their arrival soothed the mercenaries' concerns about the possibility of the authorities interrupting the proceedings. They'd come for lunch courtesy of the gentlemen of Cali.

Jorge got on a radio and equipment was brought for the mercenaries to examine: night-vision goggles, low-cost bugging equipment, Desert Eagle guns, crossbows and a sniper rifle. Tomkins rolled his eyes at the inadequate armoury. Addressing the godfathers, he drew on a list of questions that he had previously formulated. As the cartel didn't know Pablo's whereabouts, Tomkins said he couldn't act without real-time info on Pablo's location.

"How long will it take for you to find Pablo?" Gilberto said.

"With what you know: how long do you think it will take?"

"A couple of weeks."

Disturbed by their ignorance of the complexities involved in preparing for a mission, Tomkins restrained himself from shaking his head. He needed much longer than two weeks. "I'll bring a team with all the military skills required to complete this mission. These people are presently highly paid in various parts of the world. I can't calculate how long it will take to complete this mission, but we need to be paid in accordance with the risk. To finance the initial twelve-man team, I need a three-month advance payment. No matter how long the mission takes, all payments are to be for a minimum of three months, with an operational bonus payment to be discussed when the mission plan is formulated." After looking at each godfather square in the eyes, Tomkins asked for $1 million.

Without hesitating, Gilberto said that amount was no problem. If they killed Pablo, they would receive up to $3 million plus a bonus. Tomkins could barely contain his excitement. More weapons arrived in the night, including submachine guns and shotguns.

The next day, Tomkins got in a small aircraft and was flown over Pablo's Hacienda Nápoles 7,000-acre ranch. He took pictures of the huge building with terracotta roof tiles, an airstrip, two helipads, a lake, swimming pools, various other buildings for guests and bodyguards, a soccer field, a tennis court, aircraft hangars, a bullring and a massive satellite dish. The perimeter was protected by steel fencing and thatched-roof guard towers. Barriers to entry included trees, shrubs and lakes. Bodyguards lived in an L-shaped building, which contained a museum with an early 1930s Cadillac that Pablo had riddled with bullet holes to appear like Al Capone's. Surveying the location made Tomkins realise the magnitude of killing Pablo.

Tomkins left Colombia to recruit a team. He chose some ex-members of the Special Air Service (SAS) – a special forces unit of the British Army – and a couple of ex-South African Reconnaissance Commandos, some of whom he had worked with before. The younger ones were lean, fit and muscular. They weight-trained constantly and ran long distances. The older ones were stocky, worldly wise, scarred from bullets and shrapnel and hardened by battlefield experience, their bodies ravaged by combat and booze. One had a scar from knee to ankle due to an ill-fated parachute drop.

In the UK, Tomkins went on a shopping spree. Cartel money paid for bugging kits, radio scanners, frequency counters, direction-finding equipment, portable searchlights with infrared lenses, infrared markers with strobe lights visible to night-vision equipment, and medical equipment, including tracheotomy sets and inflatable splints. A security guard at Heathrow Airport let Tomkins put his bulky luggage on the plane without any questions asked. Jorge did the same at the Colombian end.

As a precaution, Tomkins told only one member of the team the nature of the mission: Peter McAleese, a former paratrooper, SAS Regiment soldier, South African Sergeant-Major and Rhodesian SAS soldier. From Scotland, built like a tank, with hardly any neck and hair, McAleese was highly respected among the mercenaries; the majority of whom had signed up for the mission on his word. He was the team leader.

Settling into apartments in Cali, the mercenaries were warned to be vigilant as kidnapping was a growth business. They were given arms, but advised not to take them outside. "We'll be moving to another place soon," McAleese said, "where we can start our training. While we're here, don't go around in more than twos or draw any attention to yourselves. You must behave in a touristy manner." At the morning meeting, McAleese chastised two men who had gone out and got excessively drunk the previous night. "Our mission is to kill Pablo Escobar," McAleese said. "It's called Operation Phoenix."

Tomkins showed pictures of Pablo and aerial photos of Hacienda Nápoles. Using maps, they planned various reconnaissance routes. Jorge said that any reconnaissance in the vicinity of Hacienda Nápoles would be immediately reported to Pablo, whose guards would swoop down on the pale-faced strangers. Using radios, the group tuned into conversations between drug traffickers and producers. The Spanish was translated by a skinny Colombian from New York who worked for the godfather Chepe.

The exotic women and disco bars in the busy city of Cali distracted some of the men. They were relocated to a heavily guarded hilltop retreat frequented by one of Miguel's wives. It included a leisure complex set on thirty acres of gardens with ornamental bridges and streams. Maintenance men tended the Japanese garden. The mercenaries swam in the pool, sweated in the sauna and had access to horse riding, tennis, indoor bowling and quad bikes. Their food was prepared by a female chef. Refraining from alcohol, they drank crates of Coca-Cola instead.

Worried that the luxury might soften the men, Tomkins and

McAleese enforced a strict discipline. At 6 am, a mandatory run around the track commenced, followed by breakfast. Then came weight-training, volleyball and other strenuous activities. To divide the men into sections, a secret ballot was held to nominate leaders. The mercenaries were instructed to write down the name of the man they would most want to be in a foxhole with during a crisis.

After a month, Tomkins was transported to the cartel's offices in a suburb of Cali called Garden City. In his typical low-key style, Gilberto ran the business from a complex of single-storey terracotta buildings. His weapons of choice were phones, fax machines, telex machines, typists and secretaries. Tomkins was escorted to a workshop which received incoming goods. Refrigerators were unpacked and their back panels removed to reveal weapons manufactured in America that had travelled via Mexico. They were hidden in the false floor of a van, which was activated by tilting the vehicle to one side.

The mercenaries were delighted with the weapons' shipment: an assortment of guns, anti-tank rocket launchers, C-4 demolition charges, ammunition and night-vision equipment. With the new arms, they performed a week of drills until everything was second nature. They practised repelling attacks by helicopters and night time raids by Pablo's men. At a remote hilltop farm, they did drills with live ammunition, machine-gunning down imaginary enemies.

On their way back with their weapons, they went to a village bar. A policeman on a motorbike noticed them and stopped. Approaching them, he observed their black combat boots. After he spoke in Spanish, one of the mercenaries' escorts from the cartel intervened. Toting a mini-machine gun in a shoulder bag, Mario was ex-army, so he displayed his military ID. The unimpressed policeman yelled in Spanish, and both men argued. Some of the mercenaries started to move towards the truck to get weapons. Jorge told them to stay put and to not do anything drastic. Mario produced a radio and made a call. A man showed up on a motorbike with a bag of cartel cash. Mario gave the bag to the policeman, who departed.

In the second month, one of the South Africans pulled out as he believed an attempt to kill Pablo Escobar was a suicide mission. Tomkins flew to England for a replacement.

The Cali godfathers hosted lunches for Tomkins, McAleese and their two chaperones: Jorge and Mario. Gilberto assured them that Pablo had been seen in many places, but Tomkins viewed the information as stale and of no tactical value.

The mercenaries stayed focused on Hacienda Nápoles. Jorge and Mario provided detailed information about the property and military and police reports on attempts to capture Pablo. After processing the info, Tomkins realised that some of his earlier assumptions were wrong. Originally, they had intended to land on the soccer field, but as they examined the photos under a microscope they spotted anti-helicopter wires on the field. The helipads were wired. The only option was to land on a tennis court.

A jungle cabin fifty miles west of Cali was transformed into a base camp. Built on wooden piles, it consisted of a big room with tables and benches, a kitchen and bathroom. Animal skulls adorned the back wall. An electric generator pumped water from the Manguido River. The cabin was equipped with a cook, a barbecue, mosquito nets, mattresses, cooking appliances, and food and drinks for the mercenaries, who arrived via helicopter. To avoid getting kidnapped by guerrillas, the men took turns on lookout duty.

A Huey helicopter arrived for the assault, which they painted emerald and white so that it appeared to belong to the Colombian police, complete with a Colombian flag under the tail rotor and Policia Nacional on both sides of the fuselage. The jungle drills included firing rockets and detonating grenades. On the beach, they shot at the river and killed imaginary enemies. They rehearsed landing at Hacienda Nápoles and bringing in additional helicopters by using coloured smoke. Yellow meant safe to land, whereas red indicated landing in hostile fire. Using maps, they chose emergency rendezvous points in case they had to evacuate the mission on foot because the helicopters had been damaged. If that happened, they would broadcast emergency radio transmissions to aircraft circling above.

They sprayed a Hughes 500 helicopter olive to match military colours and altered the doorway to accommodate a mounted machine gun. Previous raids from the air on Hacienda Nápoles had met with no resistance. Pablo's staff had even offered refreshments to the authorities. The plan was to deceive the staff with the helicopters, and to mow them down with machine guns before the mercenaries were spotted. Explosives would be dropped along the front of the main house. Upon entering the property, any locked doors would be blown open with C-4 explosives. The men received black ski masks and combat vests with special pockets to hold equipment such as grenades and radios. Backpacks were stocked with emergency supplies such as civilian clothes and medical emergency shock packs with syringes and morphine.

By the fourth month, Pablo's location was still unknown. Torrential rain trapped the men in the cabin, where they sweated blanketed by the humidity. Tomkins and McAleese were summoned to give a progress report to the godfathers at a ranch belonging to Chepe surrounded by cattle fields. Chepe's recently constructed mansion still had protective sheeting over its windows. The men arrived at a massive front door with Doric columns. About sixty bodyguards toting guns were on duty. Others were playing soccer.

Gilberto revealed that although there had been no sighting of Pablo, he knew that Pablo was going to hold a family party at Hacienda Nápoles. It would be a large affair and he would definitely be there. Although pleased that the cartel finally had info about Pablo being at a specific location at a certain time, Tomkins declined the opportunity because there would be women and children attending and they would probably get killed by machine-gun fire.

In ski masks and camouflage gear, the mercenaries resumed

drills in the vicinity of the cabin. They practised launching assaults with rockets and grenades. From helicopters, they fired machine guns at the jungle. Practising so much gave them a permanent stink of guns and gunpowder. Equipment was adjusted after weaknesses were exposed and flimsy combat vests were replaced.

Months of rehearsing as if their lives depended upon it exhausted the mercenaries. Jorge flew all of them except for Tomkins and McAleese to Panama City for a break. They partied in clubs and bars and took a scuba-diving course.

With the team absent, Tomkins and McAleese requested a meeting with the godfathers. They were transported to a luxury home, where they constructed a model of Hacienda Nápoles. They dangled aircraft from threads attached to the ceiling. They positioned helicopters on poles, so that they could replicate flights by hand. After they rehearsed the mission, they requested the presence of the godfathers.

The godfathers and four senior cartel members entered and sat down. Explaining what was about to happen, Tomkins and McAleese spoke in English, which a translator converted to Spanish. They demonstrated the assault and ended with Pablo getting killed and the mercenaries leaving safely.

Gilberto stood and clapped, immediately joined by the rest of the Colombians, which delighted Tomkins and McAleese. Speaking in limited English, Chepe told Tomkins that he would pay an additional million dollars if he fetched Pablo's head. For that price, Tomkins agreed to make room for a piece of Pablo on the helicopter.

On June 3, 1989, the mercenaries awoke as usual to the cawing of jungle birds. The men swore at each other in a comradely way. Some shared sexual fantasies. Armed with guns, they went to the river for toilet duties.

Hours later, their radio came alive in coded Spanish: Pablo Escobar was at his swimming pool at Hacienda Nápoles. Gilberto gave the go-ahead for the operation, which required two Huey helicopters. As one of the Hueys was getting repaired in Brazil,

Gilberto proposed that a smaller Hughes helicopter be used. As the lone Huey would now need to be overloaded to compensate for the missing Huey, McAleese and the pilots objected on safety grounds. Having waited a long time to get Pablo, Gilberto overrode the objections. He told the pilots to figure out how to handle the extra load. A pilot agreed that it could be done by redistributing the passengers and cargo. Gilberto ordered them to go as it might be their only chance. Gilberto announced another change. As soon as the mercenaries had landed and launched the attack, a plane was going to land on the opposite side of Pablo's ranch with over a dozen hit men sent by Pacho, who had a score to settle with Pablo.

The excitement was palpable as McAleese told the team to get ready. The animated men put on battle gear. Steel clunked and rattled as they checked their equipment, which was double-checked by another man. They tested their radios. An hour later, McAleese addressed the men with a final briefing. "I have colour-coded the areas of Pablo's mansion, which I've divided into three sections. The back of the house is black. The right of the house is red. The front is white. Once inside, the house team will advise me in the gunship which section they're in and they'll call out their position as they move. The support group will target the area one section ahead of the position of the house team. The gunship will act as an aerial stop group that can eliminate runners into or out of the building. I have 300,000 pesos emergency money for every man in case you have to make your way to an emergency rendezvous point."

Helicopter blades swooshed. The Hughes 500 helicopter buzzed like an angry bee. "Let's do it!" McAleese said. Packed into the helicopters, the men sat cramped amid weapons, explosives, ammunition and fuel tanks. Before noon, the helicopters set off on a two-hour journey to a refuel site, ten minutes from Hacienda Nápoles. The men were quiet and focused.

Eighty miles away from the refuel site, rain lashed against the helicopters. A strong wind rocked the men from side to side. The helicopters attempted to climb above the low clouds. Approaching a ridge called Silent Knife, the two helicopters separated to find the safest ways to ascend. One minute they were in a cloud, the next they could see a section of a green mountain.

Within a cloud as thick as cotton, the Hughes 500 struggled to ascend. At 8,200 feet, wind and rain tossed the helicopter around. The pilot attempted to navigate between the mountain peaks, which were suddenly visible, but a cloud filled the space and the pilot was flying blind. The dense cloud muffled the sound of the helicopter as if someone had turned the volume of the propellers down.

Crunch! The helicopter crashed. Tomkins was thrown upside down. His head throbbed with pain. The other two men who had been in the cabin were gone, and so was the helicopter door. Tree branches reached into the helicopter through the gap where the door had been.

Bracing for an explosion, Tomkins grabbed onto the branches and crawled out on his hands and knees. He ended up in a forest with no sign of anyone who had been in the helicopter. In shock and confused, he went downhill to a clearing, where he took some deep breaths to get his thoughts back under control. Gazing up, he saw the helicopter on its side, sizzling and emitting steam. Perplexed, he wondered whether he would be killed if the satchel charges exploded.

Further up the slope, McAleese limped and staggered out of the vegetation. Tomkins climbed up to help him. He found the satchel charges and cut the fuse trains and removed the detonators. Two crew members limped out of the vegetation. One's face was covered in blood. McAleese had been injured the most. He'd broken his ribs and could barely walk. Bleeding from the skull, Tomkins was afraid to touch his head in case he could feel his own brains. He suspected his rifle had caused the injury.

Noticing the pilot was absent, they scanned the area. Forging his way through the vegetation, Tomkins managed to crawl back to the helicopter, which was on its side. Entering the cockpit,

Tomkins found the pilot in a contorted position, his face deathly pale. Upon hearing Tomkins greet him, the pilot's eyes opened, but he didn't move. In Spanish, he mumbled something about his leg. Tomkins felt the pilot's leg for broken bones. It seemed OK. A wound at the back of the pilot's hips surprised Tomkins. His liver was hanging out of a torn-open torso. By moving his hand across his throat and shaking his head, Tomkins signalled to the others at the helicopter's doorway that the pilot was dying.

"You're going to be OK," Tomkins said.

In the vegetation, they searched for medical supplies among the debris, but most of it was damaged. Holding a morphine injection, Tomkins checked for a vein on the pilot's arm, but they had all collapsed from shock. The pilot's left arm had been sliced from his shoulder to his hand. Bone was jutting out. He started mumbling prayers. Several times, Tomkins stuck a needle in the side of the pilot's neck and injected morphine. Minutes later, the pilot died. Tomkins removed his dog tags, which ended up at the pilot's military funeral, where he was honoured for dying on an official anti-drugs operation.

Tomkins searched for a vein on McAleese's arms, but they had collapsed. He cut open a saline drip bag, and McAleese drank from it. They moved him to cover and tried to minimise his discomfort. They found a radio and told Jorge that they had crashed and the pilot was dead. Tomkins gave a compass bearing and draped a red towel over a shrub, so the location could be identified.

A Huey helicopter arrived, but couldn't land. It swayed in the wind. The pilot radioed that he would land at the bottom of a stream that started west of the crash. Using C-4, Tomkins started a fire for McAleese, who was trembling with pain. They insulated his bullet-proof jacket with shell dressings from the shock packs. Hoping to find a stream, Tomkins took off through the jungle canopy, mindful of the rotten trees below his feet, which acted like trapdoors. He headed towards rays of daylight penetrating the vegetation, and found himself on a cliff. Eventually, he located the stream and followed its curves down the mountain, thwarted by dense foliage. As the stream widened, Tomkins crawled downwards through the cold water, rather than battle the vegetation.

Another cliff stopped his journey. He trekked along the ridge, searching for a way down. It had been an hour since he'd left the crash site and daylight was fading. Hearing branches breaking and voices, Tomkins froze. This was Pablo's territory, and if the locals found him, they would surely take him to Pablo. The voices belonged to the other two crew members. Although relieved they were friendly voices, Tomkins was upset that McAleese had been left alone with no radio. They said McAleese had told them to go.

Fifteen minutes later, they reached another cliff. Due to zero visibility, they stopped near the edge. Soaked and cold, they couldn't sleep. Wetness prevented them from lighting a fire. Dawn brought light and the sound of a helicopter. Assuming that their rescuers were ascending the mountain, the three men entered the vegetation again, and attempted to make their way down. After four hours, they heard branches breaking below them. Armed with a submachinegun, they listened to the Spanish voices approaching. The absence of English voices made Tomkins fear the worst: they were Pablo's men. Tomkins hid.

Two unarmed peasant farmers appeared. Mario yelled at them. They identified themselves as friends sent to rescue them. The three men emerged from the vegetation and claimed to be a military operation in need of assistance to get McAleese down. Nimble like animals, the rescuers guided the men down a steep rock face covered with moss. To steady themselves, they clutched onto trees. Six hours later, they arrived at a dilapidated shack enclosed by a tree-branch fence. Hot chocolate in tin cups warmed them up.

A farmer announced that the military had arrived. Soldiers were scouring the mountainside. Tomkins assumed that the aircraft activity in the area had been spotted, and Pablo had ordered the search. Mario picked up the submachinegun and ordered everybody to leave. They abandoned the shack for the cover of the jungle and ascended the mountain at its edge, so that they could see what was happening below them.

By late afternoon, the farmers had taken them to a small valley dappled with cowpats, and into another shack. Mario and the farmers left for food and so that Mario could contact the cartel godfathers. In case Pablo's men approached, Tomkins and the other crew member found a hiding place. As the sun set, Tomkins noticed that his knee had swollen and he was caked in blood. His head was still throbbing.

After darkness, Mario and the farmers returned with food and drink. They all got in the shack and lit a fire outside of the doorway. The cold kept Tomkins awake. He worried about McAleese freezing to death on the wet mountain.

Dawn brought rain and fog. By late afternoon, the mist had cleared and a helicopter arrived. Unable to land on the rough terrain, it hovered low enough for a rescue team to jump out, armed with machetes and ropes. The three crew members scrambled on board the helicopter, which flew to a ranch airstrip. A small plane brought them to Cali, where vehicles took them to an apartment. They were greeted by Gilberto and a doctor, who gave them first aid. They showered and changed into regular clothes.

McAleese spent three nights on the mountain shivering, delirious and covered in the pilot's blood. His ribs were broken. He wrapped himself in jackets, but stayed cold. On the second night, he had an out of body experience: he floated away from his painful injured existence. Dawn snapped him out of it. He lit plastic explosives to keep warm. On the third night, he dreamt that he was in a grave. The next day, he searched the helicopter for supplies. The cold had suspended the decomposition of the pilot's corpse, which was free of flies and a grey-blue colour. McAleese found a drip and some sweets.

Back on a mountain ledge, McAleese heard Colombian voices. He grabbed a submachinegun, rolled on his stomach and prayed that Pablo's men were not approaching. As the dark hair of the first man appeared, he aimed his gun and told the son of a bitch to stop right there or else.

The man yelled amigo, and gave Jorge's name as a codeword.

McAleese lowered his gun and smiled. One of the five men poured a Pepsi down McAleese's throat. Another cut off his boots and trousers to see his injuries. They dressed him in fresh clothes. The journey down through thick jungle vegetation and waterfalls was agonising for McAleese with broken ribs and an injured back. It took over a day before he was rescued by a helicopter. He was transferred to an airplane, which Jorge piloted.

Even though the mission to kill Pablo had failed, the team was awarded an operational bonus for risking their lives. The godfathers wanted to resume the mission as their sources had informed them that Pablo was still unaware of the aborted attempt. Tomkins agreed with one condition: he would hire his own helicopter pilots. The godfathers accepted. To prevent any overloading of helicopters, they ordered two more helicopters, so that three would be available.

In June, 1989, Tomkins flew back to England, followed by two female Colombians who had smuggled money to pay for the mission. He recruited two pilots and returned to Cali, where McAleese was still recovering. In Cali, Tomkins sensed that the mission's momentum was in decline. One of the team had decided to go home. The rest were less disciplined and had formed cliques. While the team leaders stayed in Cali, the rest of the men were moved to Panama.

On August 18, 1989, the presidential candidate, Luis Carlos Galán, was assassinated. The cocaine cartels were blamed and the Colombian government cracked down on traffickers and autho-rised their extradition to America. With the authorities going from street-to-street and house-to-house hunting down anyone associated with the cocaine trade, Tomkins and McAleese were sequestered in an apartment outside Cali, which housed Gilberto and Miguel's mother. Word came down that the apartment build-ing was about to be raided, so they were transported in a Jeep around security checkpoints to another apartment.

Media around the world published the story of the failed raid on Hacienda Nápoles, putting the lives of Tomkins and McAleese in danger. They fled to Panama. The team was disturbed by the developments as they wanted to complete the mission, but now couldn't return to Colombia.

The two team members who had dropped out of the mission started doing media interviews. One was on CNN. In a UK interview, a team member's face and voice had been disguised, but when the interview was shown overseas, his disguises were lifted. He ended up shot in both knees and in a wheelchair.

Due to the government crackdown and the media leaks, the godfathers postponed the operation. In September, 1989, the team had a farewell meal with Jorge at a restaurant in Panama and flew back to England.

On September 13, the US government went public about a witness who had defected from the Medellín Cartel. It was a doctor whom Tomkins had trained during a previous mission financed by the Medellín Cartel. On a screen, Tomkins' picture was identified by the doctor, who said that Tomkins was an explosives instructor and the leader of the foreign mercenaries. He blamed Tomkins, the mercenaries and their training programs for the surge in violence in Colombia.

Two US Senate investigators showed up at Tomkins' house in England. They wanted him and McAleese to testify in Washington. Tomkins said no, and notified Jorge. The next year, they asked Tomkins to testify again at a hearing concerning arms trafficking, mercenaries and drug cartels. The Cali Cartel didn't object, so on February 27, 1991, Tomkins testified about his missions in Colombia in 1988 and 1989, including the failed attempt to kill Pablo. At the hearing, Tomkins refused to name anyone involved.

In 1991, at the US Embassy in London, the DEA told Tomkins that the US government was offering millions for Pablo's assassination. They wanted him to get hired by Pablo, so that Tomkins could kill him. With the failed attempt to kill Pablo in the news, Tomkins replied that Pablo would certainly hire him only to torture and murder him. The DEA said it hadn't thought of that.

Although Tomkins had declined the offer from the DEA, the Cali Cartel would soon require his services.

CHAPTER 5
BOMBING PABLO'S PRISON

In 1991, Pablo put more pressure on the government by kidnapping members of Colombia's elite families. One hostage was a popular TV presenter and the daughter of an ex-president. She and her family feared that any rescue attempt would be fatal as the authorities were notorious for machine-gunning everyone in such raids. Her parents urged the president to take no action. He promised that there would be no rescue attempt. But a raid happened, and she was shot fatally by the police. In public, the heartbroken mother blamed not just the traffickers, but also the president. With the public exasperated by the violence, pressure mounted on the government to reach a settlement with Pablo.

With the help of an ancient televangelist, Pablo brokered a deal to surrender to the government if they would stop extraditing traffickers to America. Upon turning himself in, Pablo was allowed to serve his time in a prison called the Cathedral, which he had built for himself. Surrounded by bodyguards, lieutenants and prison guards on his payroll, Pablo turned the Cathedral into a command centre for his cocaine empire. He equipped his quarters with luxuries and hosted parties with celebrity guests.

The guards at the Cathedral protected Pablo. The mountainside location provided a view of any potential assaults from below. Fog in the evening and at dawn provided excellent cover if Pablo needed to escape and would deter any attack by helicopter or aircraft. Pablo could easily lose his pursuers in the surrounding forest. Knowing there would come a time when he would have to flee, Pablo had buried weapons at the Cathedral.

With Pablo incarcerated in a specific location, the Cali Cartel had a direct target to strike. It was time to put the mercenaries into play again. In July 1991, Tomkins met the Cali Cartel's head of security, Jorge, in Panama City. Tomkins learned that Pablo's prison consisted of concrete blocks, a roof of asbestos sheeting, dorm-style cells and Pablo's wing. The surrounding area was booby-trapped with anti-helicopter wires, which Pablo's men only removed to allow permitted landings. Cyclone-wire netting under the roof prevented anyone getting in from above. The biggest threat though, Jorge told Tomkins, was the machine-gun posts.

As Pablo had built defences against the standard methods of assault, Tomkins was about to decline the mission. Then he considered bombing the Cathedral, using helicopters dropping drums of C-4. By remote-control detonating a couple of hundred kilos of C-4 at both sides of the building, the men inside would be cooked alive. After listening to the plan, Jorge offered one of his own. He knew a pilot who was trying to sell some 500-pound bombs. They decided to go with Jorge's plan.

Jorge flew to Guatemala to negotiate a price for four Mk-82 bombs. The seller was a colonel from El Salvador, who knew that the bombs were going to be used against Pablo. He wanted $600,000. Jorge said that sounded expensive, but he would relay it to the godfathers. Before leaving, he asked whether $500,000 was acceptable.

In need of a small ground-attack bomber, Tomkins contacted a former CIA contractor whom he had met before. He was put in touch with a seller and all three met in Miami. A deal was agreed, and Jorge arrived. The seller and his technician showed Jorge and Tomkins the plane. The lack of ID markings and the presence of a six-barrel machine gun in the nose of the plane made Tomkins and Jorge suspicious. Intending to do background checks, they filmed the seller and the technician.

Jorge left the country. Tomkins stalled the seller by paying a $25,000 deposit and arranging a meeting the next week to conclude the transaction. The seller offered Tomkins a range of military equipment, which he had not requested. The cartel established that the technician was a former DEA agent and that the seller had also been compromised.

On Sunday, Tomkins fled to England. He contacted the seller and apologised for his sudden departure. Working with US Customs as part of Operation Dragonfly, the seller tried to entice Tomkins back to inspect another plane. The former CIA contractor who'd brokered the deal was a confidential informant who received a percentage of the money or assets confiscated in sting operations.

While the bombing mission stalled for lack of a plane, Pablo was planning further attacks on the Cali Cartel. A cousin of godfather Miguel's fourth wife revealed that a family member visiting from Medellín had asked too many questions about the godfathers, including the names of their children's schools, how they were transported to school and details of other properties that the fourth wife frequented.

The godfathers sent a Cali police sergeant to arrest the inquisitive family member. The police brought the man to one of Pacho's ranches. He was escorted into a living room full of bodyguards. Sitting around with glasses of orange juice, the godfathers ceased their small talk to examine the new arrival, whose face glossed over with sweat.

In a hostile tone, Gilberto asked why the man had so many questions about their children. The captive acted clueless. Gilberto cited the questions about their children's schools. The captive claimed that he was just curious. He started to apologise for being rude.

Cutting him off, Gilberto accused him of working for Pablo. With a pained expression, the captive protested that he would never betray them. Softening his voice into a coaxing tone, Gilberto said he understood that the captive had no choice because he lived in Medellín, and Pablo had threatened him and his family. The captive fell back on his curiosity excuse.

Gilberto sprang up, demanded a fork and yelled that he was going to remove the captive's eyeballs as punishment for lying.

The bodyguards grabbed the captive and dragged him to a dining room with a large polished table. Everybody moved into the dining room. Standing at the end of the table, Gilberto demanded that the captive be brought to him. The bodyguards shoved the captive towards Gilberto. One handed the godfather a fork.

The captive broke down and sobbed. He'd done it because Pablo had threatened to kill his entire family, including his baby. He would rather die than hurt the godfathers and their families.

After resting the fork on the table, Gilberto ushered everybody back into the living room. In the dining room, the captive revealed everything to the godfathers and Jorge. He had been to the Cathedral a few times, which is where Pablo had sanctioned the fact-finding mission.

Jorge asked Miguel to intervene because the captive had details about the interior of the Cathedral, which could help the bombing mission. Miguel instructed the captive to tell Jorge everything.

Modifications to the Cathedral had started shortly after Pablo's surrender. Communications were a priority. Pablo had cell phones, radio transmitters, a fax machine and beepers. He added a bar, lounge and disco. Famous people, models, politicians and soccer players danced and cavorted there. He installed a sauna in the gym, and Jacuzzis and hot tubs in the bathrooms. In his bedroom, he had a circular rotating bed and two other beds for his family. Above his bed was a gold-framed portrait of the Virgin Mary.

The Cali Cartel was interested to learn how people and contraband were smuggled into the Cathedral. Despite rules restricting visits to official days and military police searching all of the vehicles going in and out, unofficial visitors were always circumventing the security measures. Vans with fake walls held up to twenty people. Pablo's secret visitors included politicians, judges, celebrities, models, criminals and prostitutes. Informants were kidnapped and smuggled into the Cathedral for punishments ranging from torture to execution. Large items such as computers and big-screen TVs were smuggled in by trucks laden with crates of soda, which disguised the contraband.

For emergencies and to make payoffs, Pablo kept cash in milk cans inside containers of salt, sugar, rice, beans and fresh fish, which were permitted inside because they were classified as food rations. Millions were buried near the soccer field and in underground tunnels accessible by trapdoors in the cells. His payroll was settled by helicopters flying cash out of the Cathedral.

Pablo's extensive record collection was there, including albums signed by Frank Sinatra, and Elvis records. His books ranged from Bibles to Nobel Prize winners. He had novels by Gabriel García Márquez and Stefan Zweig, a prominent Austrian writer from the 1920s. His movies on videotape included *The Godfather* trilogy and films starring Chuck Norris. Most of the prisoners had posters on their walls, whereas Pablo possessed valuable paintings. His closet was full of neatly pressed jeans, shirts and Nike sneakers, some with spikes on in case he had to flee. To thwart threats from above the prison, a remote control allowed Pablo to turn off all of the internal lights.

Further up the slope, cabins were built for privacy with female visitors and as hideouts in case the prison were attacked. They were painted brightly and had sound systems and fancy lamps. Paths were made into the forest to allow a quick getaway and to enable the prisoners to walk where the air was freshest.

As the location included a direct sightline to his family's home, Pablo mounted a telescope to watch his wife and children while talking to them on the phone. A playhouse was constructed for his daughter and filled with toys. Hidden under the playhouse was the entrance to an underground bunker.

The soccer field was renovated and night lights installed. Despite having a bad knee, Pablo played centre forward; his associates made tactful allowances such as passing him the ball to score winning goals. The professional teams who came to play against Pablo and his men were careful never to win. Pablo had a replacement on standby in case he grew tired. When he regained his energy after resting, he'd join back in. The guards served the players refreshments. Sometimes his lawyers had to wait hours to see him if he was playing soccer.

The introduction of two chefs known as the Stomach Brothers addressed Pablo's concerns about getting poisoned. He enjoyed beans, pork, eggs and rice. He'd installed exercise equipment such as weights and bikes for the prisoners to get in shape, but as they were no longer on the run and had access to endless food and alcohol, they gained weight.

The Cathedral became known as "Club Medellín" or "Hotel Escobar." *Hustler* magazine published an illustration of Pablo and his associates partying in prison, throwing darts at a picture of President George HW Bush. Pablo obtained the illustration and hung it on his wall.

When he wasn't meeting his lawyers, Pablo was usually on the telephone or reading. At nights, he sat in a rocking chair and watched the lights come on in Envigado, while thinking about his family. He took trips to watch soccer games at the stadium he'd built in Medellín. The police diverted traffic to allow his vehicles access.

Although the information provided by the captive of the Cali Cartel was helpful, Jorge wanted to get inside the Cathedral to get a feel for the place. The cartel bribed the authorities to allow Jorge onto a police helicopter that had been scheduled by Pablo to transport a judge and a court reporter to the prison.

On the morning of the flight, Jorge put on a disguise: a green jumpsuit with three stripes, indicating the rank of police captain; a big helmet with a radio microphone, sunglasses and well-polished boots. He asked the pilot to approach the Cathedral in a way that would provide the best view of the grounds. He noticed the absence of a section of perimeter fence behind the building, which the prisoners could easily escape through if attacked. Seeing the playhouse for Pablo's daughter and imagining the underground bunker, Jorge sensed that Pablo had anticipated a raid and had made preparations.

Jorge believed that the mission to bomb Pablo would end in disaster, but the godfathers were so gung-ho that he had to tread carefully. He alerted Miguel to the risks: dropping bombs on a mountainside target was far more imprecise than on flat land. Bombing what was technically classified as government property would be classified as terrorism, which could result in a government crackdown on the cartel. Miguel told Jorge to get on with the damn job.

Using the media and legal documents filed with the attorney general, the cartel leaked information about Pablo's luxuries to cause public outrage. The prison director was fired and the job was offered to a childhood friend of Jorge, who urged his friend to decline, not just because he would have no real power, but also because of the threat of the prison getting bombed. A code word was arranged, so Jorge could alert his friend if the bombing was imminent.

With the civil war in El Salvador ending, the bombs needed to be purchased quickly, otherwise the transaction would become impossible. Jorge visited Miguel to get the cash. He found the godfather meticulously wrapping $500,000. Taking possession of a red and gold box, Jorge said that it was heavy. The godfather's frown silenced him.

Jorge put the box in a shopping bag and boarded a plane. In El Salvador, a sergeant who was an aide to the colonel selling the bombs got on board. After the passengers had left, Jorge gave the sergeant $500,000. The sergeant left with the money, took $20,000 and gave the rest to the colonel.

Jorge told the officials at the airport that he was in El Salvador on business seeking opportunities in orange juice exportation. He checked into a hotel, where his passport was photocopied. The following morning, he met a local leader of the Cali Cartel's interests in El Salvador. The massive man called Nelson arranged a crew to help the mission.

At an airbase, the sergeant who had boarded the plane to get the money got in a forklift, and moved the four green bombs onto a small red truck. The bombs were disguised with straw. Accessories such as detonators were moved separately. The sergeant drove out of the compound with the bombs.

The truck travelled two miles and stopped at a busy restaurant, where Jorge was waiting with Nelson shadowing him at another table. The sergeant entered, and while walking past Jorge, he placed a key on Jorge's table. Jorge moved the key to the side of the table and left the restaurant. Nelson stood. While walking past Jorge's table, he grabbed the key. Outside, he got in the truck and left.

On the way to his hotel, Jorge stopped at a payphone. He told Miguel that they had possession of the articles. Miguel sent a plane to a landing strip on the border of El Salvador and Guatemala. Jorge told the pilot assigned to pick up the bombs that it had to be done in less than ten minutes to give the El Salvadoran authorities no time to respond to the breach of their airspace. They took note of the radio frequencies that they would use to guide the landing.

Anticipating military roadblocks, Nelson and his crew painted the bombs yellow to match the colour of the trucks and the equipment manufactured by Caterpillar that was often seen in the area. For extra camouflage, straw and four pigs were added. The mess made by the pigs would hopefully deter any thorough searches.

It was night when Jorge boarded a canoe on the Zapote River. It took him to Nelson's house. Jorge was pleased to learn that the bombs had been transported without any setbacks, but disheartened by the news that Nelson had broken a leg, making him useless for bomb loading. The pilot radioed Jorge that he was thirty minutes away. Jorge jumped on a motorbike and headed for the landing strip, followed by Nelson's men in the truck with the bombs. Jorge arrived at a dirt runway barely visible in the darkness.

The men hushed to listen for the plane. A call came on the radio that the plane was minutes away. A light from the plane on the runway exposed numerous farm animals. On a motorbike, Jorge sped to the runway to scare the animals away to prevent them from damaging the plane and destroying the mission. As Jorge revved the engine, the pigs and chickens scattered.

The plane was much smaller than Jorge had expected, generating concerns about its ability to transport bombs. It landed and the passenger door opened. To make space for the bombs, the pilot threw out empty fuel cans. The plane was so small that the crates holding the bombs wouldn't go inside. The men extracted the bombs from the crates. It took twenty minutes to get three bombs in the plane. Attracted by the commotion, local people started gathering.

The third bomb had been placed so precariously that it slipped. Not wanting to risk taking any more bombs, the co-pilot insisted that they take off. Extracting a fourth bomb from a crate, Jorge told them to wait, but the door was slammed shut. The pilot pledged to return the next day. Jorge handed the bomb accessories to the pilot, while warning him to be careful with them.

Jorge was left with a bomb, local witnesses and farm animals gazing at him, and empty fuel cans littering the runway with Made in Colombia on them. Fearful of getting caught, he told Nelson to sink the bomb in the river.

Detecting a small plane invading its airspace, Colombian air traffic control alerted the military. Two fighter planes were dispatched to intercept the plane with the three bombs. When the cartel pilot noticed the fighter planes homing in, he hid in the clouds over the mountain peaks and radioed for assistance. The cartel dispatched a second small plane. While the fighter pilots forced the decoy to land, the plane with the bombs escaped.

Jorge called Miguel from a payphone. To ensure that the landing strip had not been compromised, they decided to wait for a few days before sending a plane for the fourth bomb. Feeling unsafe, Jorge took off to Panama. He called El Salvador. Nelson's sister answered. Distressed, she said that everybody had been arrested because the authorities had discovered the fourth bomb.

She asked him where he was. Assuming that her phone had been tapped, Jorge said that he was in Costa Rica.

While Jorge sought sanctuary in a friend's house in Panama, the international news reported the discovery of a 500-pound bomb intended to kill Pablo Escobar. The news in Panama and Colombia described Jorge as a Colombian Army reserve captain involved in the plot and revealed his real name. Jorge went from being a behind-the-scenes player to making the list of men whom Pablo wanted to torture and kill. Not only Jorge, but also his family were now targets for Pablo and the authorities he controlled.

The threat of getting bombed ended the party atmosphere at the Cathedral. The prisoners evacuated the main building and moved to wooden cabins hidden in the forest beyond the soccer field at the limits of the perimeter fence. Pablo hid in a cabin in a mountain cleft, where his location was disguised from above and from the forest. It was so cold due to a spring below that he moved to another well-concealed cabin. He instructed his men to watch the sky and to shoot down anything that violated their airspace. He ordered anti-aircraft artillery and he commissioned an architect to sketch anti-bombing designs.

The architect drew a building with individual pods with bomb-proof insulation consisting of concrete and steel. Camouflaged by earth, the building would be undetectable by spy planes or satellites. Preferring to be disguised by nature, Pablo rejected the designer's extravagant plan.

The media attention had ruined the bomb plot. The godfathers hid the bombs in a storage facility and tried to keep a low profile. A US embassy cable in March 1992 stated, "The Cali Cartel is very concerned about the capabilities of the US government to interfere with their operations. They appear to be paranoid." The cable added that they were living less luxuriously, including driving cars made in Colombia.

With Pablo protected by the Cathedral, the godfathers drew up plans to kidnap his son.

CHAPTER 6
TARGETING PABLO'S FAMILY

Juan Pablo was due to enter a car race organised by the Antioquia Motorcycle League. After practising, he went to register at the event, where spectators admired his cars and asked questions. Two men appeared, who started watching him and his bodyguards. Sensing something was wrong, Juan Pablo told his bodyguards to approach the men. While they did, he sped off in a car.

Driving away, he noticed an ambulance outside the event headquarters – the same ambulance he had seen earlier on the way to school in a remote area at 7 am. To avoid it, he had made a U-turn, and now here it was again.

His father had warned that the Cali Cartel was trying to kidnap him. They intended to hold him hostage, get millions from Pablo and murder him anyway. Pablo had told his son that if either of his kids were attacked it would constitute a violation of the old-school Mafia agreement of not going after each other's family members. Pablo knew the locations and routines of all of the family members of the Cali godfathers, and up until now he had honoured the agreement. If Juan Pablo were kidnapped, Pablo would go after the godfathers' family members.

Juan Pablo was keen to participate in the race, but Pablo sent him an urgent message to come to the Cathedral. In the prison, Juan Pablo found his father sitting at a table laden with paperwork and cassette tapes. Pablo had good and bad news. The Cali Cartel definitely intended to kidnap Juan Pablo at the race, but, as usual, Pablo was on top of the situation. He had identified the kidnappers and needed Juan Pablo to remain at the Cathedral until the plot was destroyed.

The plot had two phases. The first involved soldiers, and the second, the police, who had joined forces with the Cali Cartel. Once all of the intelligence had been gathered, Pablo would contact the kidnappers. In the meantime, Juan Pablo needed to get clothes for at least ten days.

Later on, in a room with two bodyguards, Pablo had his son sit next to him on a bed. He picked up a phone and began calling the kidnappers, one by one. He told them his name and ID number. He said he knew they were going to kidnap his son at the race, assisted by the army. The plan was to attack and immobilise the bodyguards, and to drag Juan Pablo off by the hair. Pablo knew where every single one of their family members lived including their mothers. If any harm came to Juan Pablo, they and their families would have to answer to him. They'd better go ahead and evacuate their own homes because his men were under orders to take action if their family members were spotted. They had attempted to mess with Pablo's family, so now all bets were off. They had twenty-four hours to leave Medellín. If they didn't, their homes would be designated as military targets. They should be glad that Pablo had allowed them to live. Did they think that because they were the police and the military and that Pablo was in prison that he was afraid of them?

Juan Pablo stayed at the Cathedral for three weeks, while Pablo saw to it that the kidnappers lost their jobs in the police and the military.

Kiko Moncada was one of Pablo's associates in the Medellín Cartel. Pablo considered him one of his most sincere friends. When Pablo had begun to wage war, Kiko had enthusiastically pledged $100 million, which Pablo could repay anytime interest free. The money was available at his downtown office whenever Pablo needed it.

In the Cathedral, Pablo gave Kiko an update on the war with the Cali Cartel. Having used some of the money that had been offered by Kiko, Pablo asked him what was owed. Kiko summoned his bookkeeper, who extracted paperwork from a briefcase. Pablo stopped the bookkeeper and told Kiko that there was no need for such formal accounting. He just wanted to know the total, so that it could be repaid.

Kiko said that the debt was $23.5 million. He had not expected it to be paid back so soon. In fact, he had $76 million more available for Pablo. After thanking Kiko, Pablo said that he hoped he would not need it, and that he was looking forward to paying back the $23.5 million using the profits from a large cocaine shipment through Mexico. They laughed about cocaine solving all of their problems.

The Cali Cartel captured Kiko Moncada and another close associate of Pablo's, Fernando Galeano. Their freedom was granted in exchange for their commitment to cut off financial aid to Pablo. They agreed to spy on Pablo and provide information to the cartel.

When Pablo was told about their betrayal, he could not believe that such close friends had let him down. He changed his mind after listening to a recorded telephone call of one of the godfathers chastising Kiko for giving Pablo money. To test Kiko's loyalty, Pablo summoned him to the Cathedral. Pablo gave him information that he had gathered on the Cali Cartel and disclosed some plans he had made to attack the godfathers. When the plans were foiled twice by Cali hit men and police working for the Cali Cartel, Pablo knew that Kiko had told the godfathers. Pablo was aware that Kiko had acted out of fear, but that was no excuse. Kiko should have approached him immediately about the Cali Cartel.

At the same time, Fernando Galeano told Pablo that he had lost his fortune and could no longer pay for the war. One of Pablo's men found Fernando's stash of approximately $23 million.

Pablo summoned Kiko and Fernando to the Cathedral. He lectured them on everything that he'd done for them. According to Roberto Escobar, they were killed after they'd left the Cathedral: Popeye killed Kiko and Otto shot Fernando. Within days, their brothers were killed. Their distraught families begged for their corpses to give them proper burials. Pablo told them where to find them.

Pablo wanted all of the property belonging to their organisations. Their employees were told that they worked for Pablo. Their key people were smuggled into the Cathedral through a secret tunnel to attend a meeting, many of them expecting to die.

"I'm declaring an emergency," Pablo said. "Your bosses are already dead. Now you'll turn over all their resources to me. If you lie, you'll die very painfully." He reminded them that he was the boss. He said that they'd all be safe provided they paid him his dues.

The DEA recorded a version of events based on an informant's statement:

Escobar argued that while he and his close associates were in jail and needed money for their expensive war with the Cali Cartel, Galeano and Moncada preferred to store money until it became moldy rather than use it to help their friends… Escobar convinced cartel members who genuinely liked Moncada and Galeano that if the two men were not killed, the Medellín Cartel would be in a war with itself, and they would all perish.

The media reported that Kiko and Fernando had been killed in the Cathedral. Investigators sent to the Cathedral by the attorney general's office were denied entry.

Embarrassed by the murders and the way Pablo was living luxuriously in the Cathedral, the Colombian government decided to move Pablo to a new prison. When the authorities showed up at the Cathedral, Pablo assumed it was a ruse to provide the Cali Cartel an opportunity to kill him. The officials overseeing the transfer were kidnapped, while Pablo, his brother and his closest associates escaped through a gap in the fence. They disappeared into the fog and the forest.

On the run, Pablo eluded the authorities by hiding in the jungle and avoiding bombs dropped by aircraft. The resumption of the war with his many enemies reduced his vast resources. George HW Bush made Pablo the face of the enemy in the War on Drugs, and assigned multiple government agencies, including the CIA, the job of assassinating Pablo.

Throughout South America, the CIA had used death squads to get its business done. The CIA encouraged an alliance with Pablo's enemies including the Cali Cartel, which resulted in a death squad called Los Pepes – People Persecuted by Pablo Escobar. Its leaders included some of Pablo's former allies, who had once held powerful positions in the Medellín Cartel. They understood the inner dynamics of Pablo's organisation and knew many of his hiding places.

Two of the main Los Pepes' characters in *Narcos* were the Castaño brothers: Carlos and Fidel. *Narcos* gave the impression that the two rustic psychopathic Communist killers had been corrupted by exposure to the underworld of Medellín, which had lured them into cocaine trafficking. *Narcos* omitted that the Castaños were long-standing members of the Medellín Cartel.

The Castaño brothers moved deep into the killing business after the death of their father, Jesus Castaño. In the late 1970s, a guerrilla group called the Revolutionary Armed Forces of Colombia (FARC) started gathering intelligence on Jesus, a rancher in Segovia, Antioquia, who was a far right conservative and an influential local politician. The FARC had been formed during the Cold War as a Marxist–Leninist peasant force, which promoted agrarianism and anti-imperialism. Kidnapping was its primary source of income.

By 1980, Jesus had twelve children: eight boys and four girls. Ranchers bred large families, so there were more hands to work the land. The family rose at dawn to milk the cows. Jesus made his own cheese, which he sold along with milk in the town of Amalfi.

On September 18, 1981, the FARC kidnapped Jesus and demanded 50 million pesos – a gross overestimation of the 10 million pesos net worth of the Castaños. The eldest son, Fidel, 32, only managed to raise an additional 6 million.

"Believe me: I collected all the money possible and I have no way of getting any more," Fidel told the guerrilla in charge of collecting the cash.

"You are 34 million pesos short."

"If I could get more money," Fidel said, "it would only be to fight you."

Dissatisfied with the underpayment, the guerrillas tied Jesus to a tree and tortured him. Eventually, he died. The devastated siblings swore vengeance.

"What came from this was hatred," Carlos Castaño said. "A hatred that could not be banished. We decided to fight the guerrillas. But we did not realise the magnitude of the enemy and what we had embarked the entire family on. [Until then] I had never fired a shot." At the time of his father's death, Carlos was only 16.

Fidel and Carlos joined an army unit fighting the FARC. They helped guide the army through guerrilla areas. In 1982, they ascertained the whereabouts of a guerrilla, who was captured. After he was released for lack of evidence, the Castaños tracked him down to a hotel. As the guerrilla left the building, Fidel shot him dead.

Shortly thereafter, they established a death squad called "Los Tangueros," named after the family ranch, Las Tangas, where they were based. For always leading his army of over 100 men and killing without hesitation, Fidel was nicknamed Rambo.

In 1983, Carlos went to Tel Aviv to do courses in paramilitary and counterinsurgency tactics. While Carlos was out of the country, Fidel took his crusade across the province of Cordoba in north-west Colombia. Ranchers, businessmen and parts of the army supported Los Tangueros as they hated and feared the FARC for their extortion, kidnapping, and for burning farms and killing animals. In constant need of money for his troops, Fidel turned to gold-mining and land prospecting. He invested in art.

In 1983, Fidel's troops raided the villages near Segovia, where his father had been killed. The slaughtered every man, woman and child living on the river nearby. They yanked babies from their mothers and shot them. One was nailed to a plank. A man was impaled on a bamboo pole. A woman was hacked to pieces with a machete.

In the late 1980s, the Medellín Cartel couldn't get enough coca base to process into cocaine. Colombia was only a minor grower compared to Peru and Bolivia. Pablo sent Fidel Castaño to Bolivia to source more coca base. As part of the Medellín Cartel, Fidel grew rich. He controlled an area in the northern province of Cordoba, where he expanded his landholding. His well-financed death squad continue to wipe out guerrillas. Carlos stayed in Medellín, where he earned money as a hit man for Fidel and Pablo. Fidel sent his brother, Vicente, to Los Angeles to run cocaine distribution.

While Pablo was in the Cathedral, Fidel claimed that he needed a place to hide out from his enemies. Pablo gave him a room next to his own. They ate meals together and shared the same bathroom. Pablo trusted his friend until his men reported that they had caught Fidel gathering intelligence on the Cathedral. With Pablo growing suspicious, Fidel left after a few weeks.

Upon learning that some of his associates had allied with the Cali Cartel, Pablo summoned Kiko, Fernando and Fidel Castaño to the Cathedral. Suspecting that something was wrong, Fidel didn't show up to suffer the fate of Kiko and Fernando. Pablo warned his son to watch out for the Castaños because they were working with the Cali Cartel and going around saying that Pablo was killing his friends, so that he could steal their money.

Carlos Castaño documented his meetings with Gilberto in his book, *My Confession*. He wrote that he had loaned Gilberto helicopters, and that the Cali godfathers were the bosses, which was a normal type of relationship in a country like Colombia.

As well as the Castaños, numerous other traffickers abandoned Pablo. According to the DEA, "As soon as Escobar killed the Galeanos and Moncadas, their people saw themselves as vulnerable and they ran to the Cali Cartel and said, 'We want to change sides.' The Cali people said, 'OK, if you want to change sides, you need to pay us.' A lot of money changed hands."

After Pablo escaped from the Cathedral, he launched a bombing campaign and warned his family members to leave the country for their own safety.

In December 1992, Juan Pablo was in a building saying Christmas prayers with thirty other children and almost 200 adults. A bodyguard came in the room to alert them that a raid was in progress. Juan Pablo tried to escape through the back, but men with rifles blocked his path. The troops searched the congregation and requested to see their ID papers.

The plucky teenager who was big for his age identified himself as Pablo's son. He said that he lived in the building and his papers were upstairs. A police colonel arrived, and ordered two troops to guard Juan Pablo, with instructions to shoot him if he so much as blinked. The colonel called the Search Bloc's headquarters to report that he had Pablo's son and was going to bring him in.

A former governor of Antioquia who lived in the building came downstairs. Dressed in pyjamas, he asked the colonel whether the raid had been conducted lawfully. Emboldened by the governor's presence, the parents started demanding food for their children.

The colonel ordered Juan Pablo to follow him. Pablo's wife watched the guards prod her son. Separating Juan Pablo from everybody, they took him into a foyer and ordered him to stay still. Dozens of men with black hoods – including the Castaño brothers – surrounded Juan Pablo and aimed guns at him. They ordered Juan Pablo to yell his name.

The other male guests and Pablo's wife and daughter were escorted in and told to yell their names. The colonel ordered his troops to take Juan Pablo away. He protested that he hadn't done anything illegal. The colonel said they were going to have a little fun with Pablo's son at the Search Bloc's headquarters.

At 3 am, the troops escorted Juan Pablo out. An official from the inspector general's office arrived. He ordered the troops to remove Juan Pablo's handcuffs because they had no authority to arrest a minor. The official and the colonel yelled at each other. Eventually, the troops departed without Juan Pablo.

Even though they did not know that the Castaño brothers had been present, Pablo's family were in shock at the close call. They realised that they had been targeted in violation of the agreement with the Cali Cartel not to go after each other's family members. Now they would not be safe anywhere.

Pablo responded with military action, some of which he led to keep his men inspired. With fifty armed men, he organised checkpoints on roads. He set up dynamite traps for Search Bloc trucks. He took his men to the house of the head of police intelligence in Medellín, who'd participated in numerous operations against his organisation. The men arrived in vehicles, which surrounded the house. A dynamite blast reduced the building to rubble. They found the policeman still alive, so they executed him.

The authorities tried to pin the policeman's murder on Juan Pablo. A witness claimed that Pablo and his son had been seen together on the night of the murder in a bar in Envigado. In juvenile court, Juan Pablo pointed out that on the night of the murder he had been in a building that had been raided by the Search Bloc. Eventually, the witness recanted his testimony and stated that he had been tortured into making the allegation against Juan Pablo.

Pablo spent Christmas and New Year with his family, but they quickly separated again for safety reasons. He notified the attorney general that due to the raids on his lawyers, he had no choice but to concentrate on war because the legal channels for negotiating his surrender had been cut off. He criticised the violence, murder and torture by the authorities, and stated that he had formed a fighting force called Rebel Antioquia.

In early 1993, Pablo's sister-in-law, Luz, was shopping at a mall. Trucks arrived with armed men led by Carlos Castaño. Intending to kidnap her, they approached Luz, but they backtracked when they saw she was in the company of the wife of a powerful trafficker. Seeing smoke in the distance, Luz fled. Carlos Castaño and his men had set fire to her house full of art worth millions. The only piece Carlos had salvaged was Salvador Dali's *Rock 'n' Roll*. Luz reported the incident to Pablo's family, and warned that Carlos was capable of anything.

Going into 1993, the war escalated. Several of Pablo's key men were killed in battle. He ordered car bombs in Bogotá, which killed dozens of civilians and outraged the public.

The carnage was the prelude to the formation of Los Pepes. The Cali godfathers contributed $50 million for weapons, informants and assassins, in the hope of eliminating their competitor. While in America, the godfather Chepe invested in an expensive computer system that the Cali Cartel used to collect information and analyse data on the Medellín Cartel. The former Colombian president, Ernesto Samper, credited the Cali Cartel's intelligence network for being the key element in taking Pablo down.

Many members of Los Pepes were off duty police and troops who had lost colleagues and family members to Pablo. They could now torture and murder with impunity. Colombian and US government agencies – including the DEA, CIA and State Department – provided intelligence to Los Pepes.

Los Pepes' leaders were the Castaño brothers and Don Berna, who had started his career in crime as a member of a small guerrilla group called the Popular Liberation Army (EPL). He quit the guerrillas in the 1980s, and joined the Galeano faction of the Medellín Cartel. After Pablo ordered the execution of the Galeano brothers, Don Berna swore vengeance.

Pablo complained that the government was protecting Los Pepes: "Los Pepes have their torture chambers in Fidel Castaño's house [in Medellín], located… near the country club… There they torture trade unionists and lawyers. No one has searched their house or confiscated their assets… The government offers rewards for the leaders of the Medellín Cartel and for the leaders of the guerrillas, but doesn't offer rewards for the leaders of the paramilitaries, nor for those of the Cali Cartel, authors of various car bombs in the city of Medellín."

Reasoning that anyone associated with Pablo was helping to perpetuate his mayhem, Los Pepes went about systematically murdering everyone they could get their hands on, ranging from Pablo's lawyers to family members. Los Pepes blew up Pablo's mother's country house, and exploded car bombs at other family properties.

On the run, Pablo's family moved from hideout to hideout. At one, they arrived to find Pablo there. He said they needed to leave the country as soon as possible. They decided to flee to America. They booked flights for Miami scheduled to depart on February 18 at 10 am. Pablo told them to get to the airport by 5 am, but if they were recognised, the Cali Cartel and Los Pepes would be alerted.

A car transported the luggage separately the day before. The family members took taxis and shuttles to the airport to avoid attracting Los Pepes on the road. Upon arrival at the airport, Juan Pablo and his girlfriend went straight to the car with the luggage. They remained inside for three hours, unable to sleep.

When it was time to enter the airport building, Juan Pablo exited the car and realised that something was amiss. Noticing airport police in a no parking zone and a white pickup truck that Pablo had warned belonged to Los Pepes, he told his girlfriend they had been spotted. With his adrenaline surging, he insisted they quickly go through passport control to get in a safer area. The long queue was untenable, so they bolted to the front with the other people in line yelling at them.

In a booth, a DAS agent studied Juan Pablo's passport, which had been signed by Pablo because his son was a minor. Eventually, he reluctantly stamped both passports. Beyond the booth, Juan Pablo noticed hooded figures lurking behind tinted windows, carrying machine guns and rifles. The airport staff were tense as if bracing for the hooded men to take action. No officials or police approached the men.

The rest of the family members joined the line for the metal detector and drug-sniffing dogs. Young men appeared with their suitcases and started opening them for inspection by Elite Antiterrorist Unit agents. With onlookers marvelling at the drama, Juan Pablo protested that the agents shouldn't be ripping their luggage open just as they were about to board a plane. Undaunted, the agents kept repeating the same searches to make the family miss their flight, so that Los Pepes could intercept them on the way out.

Juan Pablo hand-signalled to a bodyguard who was shadowing the family. An agent noticed, but the bodyguard disappeared. Juan Pablo protested that he had only been itching his ear.

After the plane left without them, they were told to leave immediately. Pointing at the hooded men outside the windows, Juan Pablo said that the agents had delayed the family on purpose, so that Los Pepes could abduct and kill them. The agents were now responsible for their lives, and if anything bad happened to them, Pablo would hold them accountable. The prospect of retribution from Pablo frightened the agents.

The media arrived with lights and cameras flashing. The hooded men disappeared. A fifty-year-old airline worker approached Juan Pablo and offered to help. He took Juan Pablo to an office with a phone and a *Yellow Pages*. They ordered a helicopter. But when it arrived, agents blocked the family from boarding it.

The bodyguard whom Juan Pablo had signalled had alerted an official from the inspector general's office, who finally showed up. The inspector ordered the agents to release the family. They had too much luggage for the helicopter, so they abandoned it.

A colonel from the Search Bloc told Juan Pablo that they were going to find and kill his bastard father. Juan Pablo wished him luck. The colonel clenched his fist as if to throw it at Juan Pablo, but changed his mind upon noticing the media cameras. The colonel said that Juan Pablo would not be so lucky next time, and that they would all be killed.

The helicopter took them to another airport, where a member

of the inspector general's office was waiting to help them. The media showed up again. The family waited in an office, while Juan Pablo devised a plan to dodge Los Pepes, which he assumed was on its way. Juan Pablo announced to the reporters that the family had almost been killed in an ambush at the previous airport. He needed their help in exchange for an interview. They were going to leave the building, but they needed the media to follow them and to keep filming in case they were abducted.

At high speed, the family in a taxi, followed by the media, headed for the building that the Search Bloc had raided during the pre-Christmas celebrations. In the basement, Juan Pablo gave his first media interview. He discussed their situation and the prospect of Pablo surrendering to the authorities. After the interview, the family fled through an escape route by the swimming pool. They traversed a small creek to get in the backyard of the next property, where they owned an apartment and a getaway vehicle. After they had sped off in an SUV, five trucks arrived and hooded men emerged. Los Pepes searched everywhere for the family.

At another property, they changed clothes and vehicles. They ended up at an apartment, where they found Pablo's wife upset, having listened to the news report the failure of their attempt to leave the country. Juan Pablo was warning the family that the new location was unsafe, when someone rang the doorbell. A bodyguard sent by Pablo confirmed that they had to leave immediately.

The apartment had been compromised, so they needed to extract all the money hidden there. They tried to undo the screws for the wardrobe containing the money, but they were too tight. If they broke it open, the neighbours might have reported the noise. Assuming that by the time the authorities had arrived, they would be gone with the money, they took a hammer from the kitchen and smashed the wood. They packed the money into a briefcase and fled.

Driving away, they scoured the area for hooded men. Their car snaked across town on a convoluted route to shed any tails. Pablo had opened the garage door. As soon as the car was inside, he closed it. Relieved they had dodged Los Pepes, he hugged them. He told them that he had been watching everything on TV and listening on a radio. He praised Juan Pablo for his quick thinking and for evacuating them in a helicopter.

As part of a strategy to keep Pablo's family in constant danger from Los Pepes to draw Pablo into making a mistake, the US government cancelled their visas, so that they couldn't flee to America. In late February, Pablo assured his family that he would make arrangements for them to go to another country, even if it meant getting fake documents and false visas. The alternative was they could join him in the jungle, where he had the support of the ELN guerrillas. Unable to bear the thought of their children in the jungle, his wife sobbed.

In late February and early March, Los Pepes went on a killing spree, wiping out more family members, employees and lawyers. Most of Pablo's long-standing bodyguards had either died or surrendered to the authorities. He had never been more isolated or had to depend on so few people. With the authorities conducting so many searches in Medellín, Pablo left for a few days, and returned to take his family to a new hideout.

On April 15, a car bomb exploded in Bogotá, causing multiple casualties in a shopping area. In response, Los Pepes increased their kidnapping and killing.

On May 25, Pablo organised a celebration for his daughter's ninth birthday by arranging horseback riding. Two men approached Juan Pablo's girlfriend, and asked if she was the wife of Fabio Ochoa, a senior member of the Medellín Cartel. Spooked by the men, she notified Pablo, who ordered everybody to pack their things.

With the horses loaded with luggage, guns, cash and a birthday cake, they traversed a mountain. The rain increased, as did the gradient of the slopes. A horse fell over and slid backwards towards the family. The family members only just jumped out of the way in time to avoid the animal. On the other side of the mountain, they eventually arrived at a hideout, soaked from the rain.

In the house, insects and cold and damp kept them awake. They used hairdryers to heat the beds up. Pablo's inability to protect his family was apparent, so he offered encouraging words about joining the guerrillas in the jungle. He claimed to have bought a position as a guerrilla commander for $1 million. In the jungle, he would be safe. It would allow him to rebuild his cocaine empire. It was his only option as the government had refused to negotiate.

In June 1993, Pablo's brother-in-law Carlos arrived home from the Caribbean and was kidnapped by twenty-five hooded men near an airport in Medellín. After torturing him, Los Pepes shot him multiple times in the head and ditched his body on the outskirts of Medellín. Watching the news on TV, Pablo's wife sobbed. In *Pablo Escobar: My Father,* Juan Pablo claimed that Carlos had never been involved in violence and had earned a living selling mops.

After a psychic predicted that Pablo would die that year, Pablo located the psychic and provided his family's dates of birth and other information to get more predictions.

In September, Pablo said goodbye to his family, so that they could go under government protection. They lived sparsely in a house with armed agents. Their protection had been agreed with the attorney general, with whom Pablo was negotiating his surrender. One night, trucks with hooded men showed up and started firing at the building. The twenty agents protecting them were too afraid of Los Pepes to retaliate. As bullets slammed the walls, the family hid in the house.

The next day, the agents reinforced the house with sand bags to buffer future attacks. Their number doubled to forty and more heavy-duty weapons arrived. A siren was installed on the roof. It was quickly tested, when hooded men arrived in two cars and started firing with rifles. The family dashed into the recesses of the house to take cover. With rifles, machine guns and handguns, the agents took their positions and returned fire.

The escalating danger helped to motivate Attorney General de Greiff into being more forthcoming with helping the family leave the country. He sent a message stating that he was looking for a country which would accept them. He would do so on the basis that he would trust Pablo to turn himself in.

With technology and intelligence provided by the US agencies, Los Pepes and the Search Bloc were homing in on Pablo's whereabouts. While Pablo was on a call with his son, they traced his location and launched a huge manhunt. Pablo rushed from his hideout on a mountain and dashed along cliffs in the darkness and the rain. Fleeing from his pursuers, he dropped his torch and radio. He was convinced he would die, but the troops were too afraid of falling over the cliff to follow him. Caked in mud, he showed up in a neighbourhood and got in a taxi.

In October 1993, one of Pablo's few remaining bodyguards was reported as having died in a shootout with the police, which was a euphemism for assassination. Upon hearing the news, Juan Pablo struggled not to cry as he knew his father's days were numbered.

The family had communicated with Pablo through notes smuggled out of their government-protected home. The people carrying the notes included Pablo's daughter's nanny, a teacher of Pablo's children and other staff. One staff member was granted time off to see his son on Halloween. Juan Pablo advised him to leave the building surreptitiously by going over a creek. Not wanting to get his shoes wet, he refused. Instead, he had the agents drop him off on a main road and he got in a taxi. He was never seen again. Hooded men smashed the door down on a building and snatched the kid's teacher. Her corpse was never found.

Realising that Los Pepes would target the nanny next, Juan Pablo called her home. Her son said that she had just left for a taxi. Juan Pablo ordered him to drop the phone and chase her as fast as he could because the taxi was a trap. When he got back on the phone, he was devastated. The nanny was gone.

Worried about a remaining bodyguard, Juan Pablo sent a house cleaner to warn him. Approaching the house, she saw several cars with Los Pepes. The bodyguard shot at the hooded men, but there were too many. They shot him non-fatally, and took him away to be tortured.

With nearly everyone associated with Pablo now dead or in prison, the main targets left were Pablo's immediate family. But they were worth more to Los Pepes alive because they were the ultimate bait to draw Pablo out of hiding. The US agencies such as the CIA were banking on Pablo finally exposing himself as the threat level from Los Pepes intensified.

Worried that their government protectors could grant Los Pepes access to them at any time, the family slept on mattresses in a room with Juan Pablo guarding them with a gun left by one of Pablo's bodyguards. Unable to communicate with Pablo because all of the messengers were dead, the family suffered some of its darkest days.

The attorney general sent a message that Pablo had to turn himself in before he would allow them to leave the country.

The threat from Los Pepes motivated the family to try to flee to Germany without the government's consent. They sent an anonymous person to purchase tickets for Frankfurt. But the attorney general found out, and filed criminal charges against Juan Pablo to prevent him from leaving. The charges were transporting illegal drugs and sexually assaulting young women. Juan Pablo protested vehemently against the charges. He pointed out that he had a girlfriend and as Pablo's son he had never been short of potential dates. The attorney general's office pressed the issue of him bringing a box of guns into the building. Juan Pablo granted permission for the building to be searched.

The attorney general's office dropped the charges, but issued a death sentence by stating that the bodyguards provided by the government were going to be removed in the next few days. Pablo's wife screamed at the officials for threatening to leave her children unprotected and at the mercy of Los Pepes.

In late November, the family boarded a flight to Frankfurt from Bogotá. US agencies intervened. Germany denied them entry. They were escorted onto a flight back to Colombia. On November 29, the government transported the family from the airport to an apartment in Bogotá, which was the only place that the attorney general's office could guarantee their safety.

Pablo had been watching the news broadcast his family's ordeal. He made several calls to them while they were in a meeting with some generals, but upon recognising his voice, Juan Pablo kept referring to him as grandma, stating that the family was OK, and hanging up out of concern that the calls would be traced.

After the family's meeting with the generals, Pablo got on the phone with his wife. Crying, Maria Victoria said that the family needed him, so he must take good care of himself. He said that his motivation in life was to fight for them. He claimed to be ensconced in a cave, and that the hardest part of their struggle was over.

On a separate call to his son, Pablo agreed to answer media questions. Despite his son's warnings of staying on the phone for too long, Pablo dropped a discipline that had kept him alive for over twenty years. On a later call, Pablo dictated five answers. Abruptly halting the conversation, Pablo said that he would call his son right back.

Technology had tracked the call to a house by a shopping centre. Armed men descended on the location and teemed around it, preventing any escape. The front door was smashed down. The first shots were fired at an empty garage with a taxi that Pablo had used to drive around making calls. Pablo's lone bodyguard made it to an orange-tile roof. A spray of gunfire from the rear of the house sent him flying onto the grass.

Seeing what had happened to his bodyguard, Pablo tossed his sandals and stayed against a wall on the roof. Hoping to escape down a back street, he moved along the wall. The gunfire was so intense from all sides of the house that it tore up the bricks and the roof and some members of the raid thought they were under attack by Pablo's bodyguards and radioed for help.

After Pablo fell, the shooting stopped.

"It's Pablo! It's Pablo!"

Troops approached the blood-soaked corpse and flipped it over.

"Viva Colombia! We've just killed Pablo Escobar!"

"We won! We won!"

Pablo had been shot three times. A bullet entered his thigh above the knee and emerged below his kneecap. Another went in below his right shoulder and got stuck between two teeth in his lower jaw. The third went into the right ear at the centre and came out in front of his left ear, slicing through his brain, killing him instantly.

Who fired the kill shot is still debated. In *Killing Pablo*, Mark Bowden claimed that Pablo was assassinated by the Search Bloc after he had been floored by the first two shots. The shooter had probably stood over Pablo, and would have been sprayed with blood. Steve Murphy of the DEA claimed that a few hours after Pablo's death a member of the Search Bloc had offered to sell his shirt and trousers for $200 because they were stained with Pablo's blood. Years later, the chief of intelligence for the Colombian National Police claimed that Pablo had been killed at close range because nobody had wanted to risk the disaster that would have arisen if he had been captured alive. He compared Pablo to a trophy at the end of a long hunt. According to the official reports, a sergeant who died two years after Pablo's death, along with a police chief and another officer, were the only three who shot Pablo.

The *Narcos* good-versus-evil myth is based on the official account. It showed General Martinez' son spotting Pablo on the phone and radioing for backup. The troops and the DEA's Steve Murphy chased Pablo through the house. Attempting to flee, Pablo was shot by a soldier with a rifle. He was on his back, panting. Then another soldier finished him off at close range. Walking away from the scene, Steve Murphy noticed the Castaño brothers and Don Berna lurking around, which barely acknowledged the role Los Pepes played at the end of the hunt, but gave a clue that much more had happened than in the official account.

While serving over 30 years in federal prison for drug trafficking, Los Pepes' Don Berna wrote a book that was published in 2014. In *How We Killed the Boss,* he claimed that he and his brother known as Seed and other members of Los Pepes were present at the raid. They had accompanied the special forces on orders from a lieutenant. When Pablo ran from the house onto the roof, Seed had aimed his rifle and shot Pablo in the head. The commander and the other troops had hugged the brothers, while shooting into the air and yelling, "Viva Colombia!" Los Pepes had to leave before the media arrived because the authorities didn't want to be associated with the notorious death squad.

General Martinez – the head of the Search Bloc at the time – denied Don Berna's claim: "It's not true what he says. I was constantly communicating by radio with police officer Hugo Aguilar and with Lieutenant Hugo Martinez Bolivar, my son, and the operation was carried out entirely by policemen."

In the book *Escobar*, Pablo's brother Roberto described the police barging in downstairs and Pablo sending his bodyguard to investigate. Shot multiple times, the bodyguard died while Pablo made it to the roof, looked around and saw that he was surrounded. Having pledged never to be captured or killed, he shot himself in the head to deprive the government of being able to claim that it had murdered him.

Juan Pablo wrote that he had overheard his father on a radiophone to a bodyguard stating that he would never allow the authorities to take him alive. Pablo told his son that when the inevitable showdown came he would fire fourteen rounds from his Sig Sauer pistol, leaving one to shoot himself in the right ear. The photo of Pablo on the roof shows Pablo next to his Sig Sauer pistol, which had been fired. Pablo's Glock was still holstered. Even *Narcos* showed Pablo's blood-soaked right hand, which would have arisen from the spray if he had shot himself in the ear. Juan Pablo is convinced that his father honoured the suicide pledge.

Within minutes of Pablo's death, a special forces agent notified the Cali Cartel. An ecstatic Miguel told his head of security, Jorge, that Pablo was dead and gave his terrified accountant a bear hug. Teary-eyed Miguel called Gilberto. The brothers almost cried with relief. Their bodyguards took to the streets, honking horns and firing guns. Jorge advised them to celebrate in a private way. With the godfathers footing the bill for the alcohol, the cartel workers danced into the night to South American music, ecstatic that the war with Pablo was finally over.

In celebration of Pablo's funeral, Gilberto hosted a party for 200 people. Hearing loud music in the middle of the night, a military patrol went to investigate and found numerous bodyguards protecting the parked cars. The commanding officer ascertained that no permit had been issued for the event, which was creating commotion. Troops charged into the house, blocked the exits and turned off the music. The revellers were lined up and ordered to show ID before being allowed out of the front door.

Trapped in the house, Gilberto knew that if he were arrested, he might end up incarcerated for years on trafficking charges. Taking advantage of the chaos, the Chess Player disappeared into the kitchen. Spotting an armed guard at the exit, he came up with an escape plan. He took a scoop of the soup on the stove and spilled it over his face, beard and clothes. Covered in a bright red stain and with his beard littered with morsels of food, he stumbled towards the back door and burped. The guard ordered him to go back inside. Gilberto said that if he didn't leave immediately, his wife would kill him. Shaking his head, the guard refused to allow Gilberto out. The godfather extracted his penis and urinated on the guard. The angry guard grabbed Gilberto and threw him outside into the darkness. Gilberto escaped.

CHAPTER 7
WAR REPARATIONS

Around the same time that Miguel had received word of Pablo's death, a news reporter called Juan Pablo. She said that the police had killed Pablo at Medellín's Obelisco shopping centre. Having talked to Pablo less than ten minutes ago, seventeen-year-old Juan Pablo found her claim unbelievable. In shock, he demanded to know what Pablo was doing at a shopping centre as it was a strange place for him to be. The reporter insisted that it had been confirmed. Juan Pablo's girlfriend turned on the radio. The broadcaster said that Pablo had died in a police operation.

In a statement to the reporter, Juan Pablo exploded on his father's enemies. He was going to murder the fuckers who had killed his father. He would kill the bastards himself. After refusing to comment any further, he hung up and sobbed. With the whole family crying hysterically, Juan Pablo imagined how he would destroy his enemies: he would become even more dangerous than Pablo.

As his emotional reaction subsided, Juan Pablo saw the error of pursuing the gangster lifestyle. He remembered the stress that Pablo had caused his family, and all of the people who had died, including many family members and close friends. He could not go down the same road as his father. He regretted vowing revenge. His father's incensed enemies would have heard his statement to the reporter, and would now be plotting to kill him. Hoping to undo the damage, Juan Pablo contacted a TV station and announced that he would not seek revenge. His only care was his family's safety. They had all suffered. He wanted to work hard to promote peace.

After Pablo's death, the first family member to get attacked was Roberto Escobar. On October 7, 1992, Pablo's brother had surrendered to the authorities, not knowing whether they would kill or incarcerate him. For ten days, he slept on the floor of a little cell. Charged with illegally escaping from the Cathedral prison, he was facing a maximum sentence of 58 years.

A month later, he was moved to the maximum-security Itagüí prison, where he was treated more like an inmate than an animal. A lawyer – whom Los Pepes subsequently murdered – brought him a TV with a mobile phone inside to communicate with Pablo during his final year alive.

On December 2, 1993, Roberto was in his cell when the radio announced Pablo's death. Finding it hard to accept, he sobbed. Upon hearing Juan Pablo lash out at Pablo's enemies, Roberto called him, urged him to remain calm like his father did in dangerous moments and suggested that he make a public statement apologising for his outburst.

A few weeks passed in a blur as Roberto mourned the loss of his brother and his legal woes receded into the background. At nights on his bunk, he reminisced about childhood times with Pablo, their days together at Hacienda Nápolés and their many close escapes from the law. Roberto prayed for his brother and dreamed about him.

On December 18, Roberto attended the prison church to pray for Pablo. After speaking to the priest, he headed back to his cell. A guard said that a letter had arrived from the prosecuting attorney. Roberto asked where it was. Pointing towards a small room, the guard said that the letter was in there and Roberto needed to go inside the room to read it.

As a precaution, Roberto usually paid someone to open his mail. But on this occasion, a guard handed him a letter with the official prison system initials and seals from the control posts. Convinced the envelope contained a response to an appeal he had made, Roberto was keen to find out the result. Picking up the envelope, he noticed its heavy weight.

Tearing it open exposed a green wire. Before he could react, a letter bomb exploded in his face. The force of the blast under his chin propelled him upwards until his head hit the ceiling, which cracked the tiles. Unable to see anything, it felt as if his eyeballs were gone. Smelling blood, he prayed to stay alive.

With the guards on the payroll of the Cali Cartel, no one came to help Roberto. Crawling on the floor, trying to find the door, Roberto realised that the blast had peeled off the flesh from the fingers on his right hand. Dragging himself, he heard people shouting his name. For a few hours, Roberto was left in a room with no medical treatment. He assumed that the guards were waiting for him to die. Blind and vulnerable, he worried about somebody coming to finish the job.

Finally, a doctor friend who had visited earlier that day showed up with painkillers. He cleaned up the blood and took Roberto to a clinic, where they saved his life. His family members arrived, but were ordered to leave for their own safety. His mother refused: if Roberto died, she would die with him.

After examining the remains of Roberto's eyes, the doctor wanted to remove them as he believed that his vision would never return. An eye infection could kill him. Also, Roberto's nose had been shredded, his face and hands burned, his hearing damaged and he had shrapnel all over his body.

"Roberto Escobar is in a state of consciousness with multiple injuries from an explosion," a hospital spokeswoman told local radio. She said that he would undergo surgery on his eye and that his injuries had "put his life in danger."

After preventing the doctor from removing his eyes, his mother set about searching for another doctor. She settled on a military doctor who treated soldiers who had been badly injured fighting guerrillas. Roberto was moved to Medellín, where he endured twenty-two operations.

After receiving a cornea transplant, Roberto should have been put on bed rest to ensure the success of the operation, but he was transported back to the prison and denied eyedrops. The transplant failed. Other sabotage attempts were made on his recovery.

One nurse put alcohol on his eyes, causing an unbearable burning sensation. When he was returning from an operation, the guards dropped his stretcher.

No one was held accountable for the bomb, which had managed to get through five different checkpoints in a maximum-security prison with bullet-proof doors, guarded by the police, the army, the DAS and prison guards, who had cameras, x-ray machines and metal detectors. One x-ray machine had conveniently malfunctioned an hour before the letter had arrived. The Colombian authorities claimed to have investigated three guards who had handled the package. The US Embassy in Colombia concluded that although no one had claimed responsibility for the explosion, Los Pepes was the main suspect.

Pablo's daughter, Manuela, eight years old, went on TV to ask Los Pepes to stop the violence against her family. She asked the president to allow them to leave the country. "What have I done for this to be happening to me?"

Pablo's family members asked the US embassy to house them in Florida, but the DEA boss in Colombia said that even if they provided enough information to incarcerate the entire Cali Cartel, they would still not receive a visa.

In the aftermath of Pablo's death, there was a scramble for his fortune. One thing that kept Pablo's family members alive was that his debtors needed them to locate and hand over assets. At a meeting in a prison, Juan Pablo was told by a powerful kingpin that Pablo owed him $1 million. After verifying the debt, Juan Pablo paid the kingpin with one of Pablo's planes and its spare parts.

At the La Modelo prison, Maria Victoria and Juan Pablo went to meet one of Pablo's trafficker associates, who had a message from the Cali Cartel. Nervously, Juan Pablo took a keychain with a little baby Jesus on it and wore sunglasses to disguise himself from assassins. According to his bodyguard, he was about to go through one of the hardest times of his life. Inside, they were greeted by Popeye, one of Pablo's most prolific hit men. Popeye said nothing bad would happen in the prison, and that the trafficker was his son's godfather.

They were escorted to the trafficker's cell. The three men inside were quickly joined by four more. With a deadly glint in his eyes, the trafficker introduced himself. In a stern tone, he said that everybody knows who won the war, and that the new boss of bosses was Gilberto. Pablo's family needed to go to Cali to resolve things with the godfathers. Firstly though, the godfathers had requested an act of good faith: Juan Pablo needed to drop his formal complaint with the attorney general's office whereby he had alleged that the Cali godfathers had ordered the bombing of the Monaco building in 1988. Juan Pablo didn't have a problem dropping the allegation, but the prospect of going to Cali terrified the teenager. He didn't want to risk getting killed. Scowling, the trafficker asked who Juan Pablo thought he was refusing to go to Cali. The bodyguards protecting Pablo's family were awaiting orders from Cali to assassinate them all for just 300 million pesos. He could make the call right now to have them killed. After his wife arrived, the trafficker said they all needed to leave his cell so that he could have sex.

Outside the cell, Juan Pablo felt a hand on his shoulder and jumped. "Follow me," said a tall man. After guiding them to a quiet corner in the prison building, the man said that Juan Pablo's fear of going to Cali was natural. The godfathers had experienced so much violence from the war with Pablo that they wanted it to end just as much as Pablo's family desired peace. If they refused to go to Cali, the godfathers would have them killed. The arrangements had been made. Going to Cali might just save their lives. Instinctively trusting the stranger, Juan Pablo asked what his role was in all of this. The man said that he had been an enemy of Pablo, who had caused him lots of problems. He was in prison awaiting extradition to America.

A few days later, Juan Pablo met a lawyer, who asked him to state that Pablo had insisted on him making the Monaco bombing allegation about the Cali godfathers without any proof of them having conspired to do so. A prosecutor arrived with a secretary to take a statement. The cartel lawyer waited upstairs. Juan Pablo sensed that they knew he was acting under pressure. After finishing the statement, Juan Pablo received a copy. The secretary called somebody to report that everything had been settled.

The next time that Juan Pablo visited the La Modelo prison, the trafficker who had urged him to go to Cali was drunk. He showed Juan Pablo a box containing fifty watches, and insisted that Juan Pablo have one that had cost $100,000.

During the prison visits, a meeting with the Cali godfathers was organised. *Narcos* showed Pablo's wife meeting Gilberto on the same day that Pablo had died, with Los Pepes singing and dancing in an adjacent room, but nothing had been arranged so quickly. The godfathers were far more cautious than that.

Before Juan Pablo could leave for Cali, the godfathers wanted to receive a visit from Roberto Escobar's lawyer and Popeye's girlfriend. Another woman put forward for the visit refused to go because she was afraid of getting murdered in Cali. In Cali, the two visitors told the godfathers that Pablo's family and his workforce wanted peace. Without conceding much, the godfathers expressed interest in negotiations.

A few days later, a senior member of the Cali Cartel arrived at Pablo's family's apartment and demanded to be let in. Demonstrating the reach of the Cali Cartel, the government-appointed bodyguards didn't search him. Over lunch, he said that they would be allowed to live, but the price would be steep as the godfathers were looking to recuperate the costs of the war against Pablo plus interest. The visitor had paid $8 million towards the war, which he wanted back.

In January 1994, a distressed relative who had never been involved in the drug business arrived at Pablo's family's apartment from America. For years, he had lived overseas with his family to avoid the war. At home, he had received a call – on a number he'd kept private – from Miguel, who had instructed him to come to Cali. Attempting to stall Miguel, the relative had responded that he needed a few months to arrange things before he could return to Colombia. Miguel gave him four days to arrive in Cali, otherwise he would be tracked down. Terrified, the relative had quickly come to Bogotá en route to Cali. Pablo's family urged him to avoid Cali. He said that hiding from the godfathers was impossible. They would find him anywhere in the world.

The next day, the relative checked into Cali's InterContinental Hotel, where the employees were on the cartel's payroll. The white high-rise with marble floors in its reception provided guests with spectacular views of the Cali River. It had an outdoor terrace with a pool and a full-service spa. It was popular with wealthy businessmen and tourists, who were attended by a plethora of waitresses and bellmen.

The relative was chauffeured to an opulent home. Inside, the godfathers were waiting. Miguel said they had researched the relative's background. They were satisfied that he could negotiate directly with the family. Many people had died unnecessarily in the war with Pablo. The godfathers wanted to address the root causes of the war, which required Maria Victoria to come to Cali. Realising that he wasn't going to be murdered, the relative relaxed. He would arrange for Pablo's wife and son to come to Cali. Gilberto cut him off: Maria Victoria must come alone because Juan Pablo was just a little boy who should be hiding under his mother's dress; Juan Pablo ate and walked like a duck, just like Pablo. Despite Gilberto's attitude, the relative returned to Bogotá full of hope of a settlement. He wanted to return to Cali with Maria Victoria immediately.

Going to Cali required outsmarting the attorney general's office, which was protecting Pablo's family. Maria Victoria asked her psychologist to grant an extra-long session to treat her depression. During that time, she would disappear to Cali. After the psychologist agreed, Maria Victoria fled down the fire-escape stairs. The relative was waiting in a van.

In Cali, the relative called Miguel, who instructed them to stay at one of his hotels while he notified the other godfathers.

Almost a day later, just before 10pm, Miguel arrived to get them in a car driven by his head of security, Jorge. Dressed in mourning clothes, Pablo's wife met Jorge in the lobby. He greeted her, took her outside and opened the door. He said that the meeting was fifteen minutes away. Inside, Maria Victoria fumbled with her purse. Noticing her nervousness, Jorge suggested that she try and relax. Unarmed, Jorge drove cautiously, occasionally checking the mirrors to see if they had been tailed.

The car arrived at the iron gates of a luxury property protected by armed men. Jorge parked. Maria Victoria emerged. A guard searched her purse. She followed Jorge into the house through various rooms and into a poorly lit office. Maria Victoria entered a room in which forty senior traffickers were seated.

At a large table were the godfathers, Carlos Castaño of Los Pepes, and representatives of the Moncada and Galeano families, formerly of the Medellín Cartel, but whose leaders Pablo had ordered killed when he was in the Cathedral. On leather chairs, the godfathers squinted with displeasure at Maria Victoria. Greetings were absent. Scowling at her from the other side of the table, Gilberto instructed her to sit in an empty chair next to Miguel at the centre of the large table. The relative who'd arranged the meeting sat at the end of the table.

"What do you have to say?" Gilberto said with accusation.

Addressing them as gentlemen and clutching a bottle of water, Maria Victoria said the war was over. She had come in the hope of reaching an agreement to save the lives of her children and everyone else associated with Pablo.

For ten minutes, Miguel lambasted Pablo for costing them all over $10 million, which they wanted back. They had listened to all of the conversations recorded during the war, and had heard Pablo's siblings demanding an escalation of the violence. His siblings, including his brother Roberto, would get no leniency from the godfathers. They warned her that Pablo's mother was her enemy. As his outburst drew to a close, Miguel said that he wanted to know whether Pablo's family was genuinely seeking peace.

Other traffickers took turns to rail against Pablo and to make claims on what they were owed due to the war. One said that Pablo had wiped out two of his brothers. Another had been kidnapped and had paid over $2 million plus some real estate to obtain his freedom. Pablo had burned down a trafficker's ranch. To avoid getting kidnapped, he had remained out of the country for years. One said that if things were reversed – if Pablo had won the war and their wives were petitioning him for mercy – then Pablo would probably have done something horrible to them because he was an evil man. Maria Victoria said that it was due to God's wisdom that she was there, and not their wives.

Carlos Castaño said that he had searched everywhere for Maria Victoria and her daughter because he had planned on chopping them up into little pieces and sending them to Pablo in a sack.

Taking charge again, Gilberto said that everybody present was willing to make peace with everyone concerned except for Juan Pablo. Maria Victoria wept. She would never find peace without her son. She offered to guarantee his actions with her life and for them to permanently leave Colombia. Gilberto said that many of the men present were concerned that Juan Pablo would end up wealthy and in a position to enact revenge. He could finance an army and resume war. There could only be peace if the women lived and Juan Pablo died.

In a calm tone, Miguel said that the recorded conversations had shown that Maria Victoria had been a voice of reason. She had tried to calm Pablo down and de-escalate the war. Numerous times, she had asked Pablo to make peace. Because of these actions, she was there today. On the other hand, she had supported an evil man until the end. She had written love letters even though Pablo was constantly unfaithful. In a respectful tone, he added that their wives had listened to the recordings as an example of how a woman should support her husband. Miguel wanted her to get Roberto and Pablo's men in prison to pay $6 million, which they owed. The total owed to everybody in the room was $120 million. They wanted paying in cash. She had ten days to present a payment plan. The room fell silent. The meeting ended.

On the ten-hour trip back to Bogotá, Maria Victoria was overcome by exhaustion. Unable to converse, she sobbed relentlessly. Back in the apartment, she told Juan Pablo what had happened, including the godfathers' decision to kill him. She added that Pacho was the only godfather who had not demanded compensation.

To satisfy the godfathers' demands, an inventory of the family's assets was made. Pablo had bought expensive paintings, including art by Salvador Dali, Pablo Picasso and the Colombian painter Fernando Botero. Upon learning that Pablo had some of his art, Botero expressed dismay, but, years later, Botero felt inspired enough to paint *The Death of Pablo Escobar*, which included Pablo in Botero's signature rotund style, on a roof, gun in hand, with a hail of bullets shoving him backwards. Maria Victoria documented the condition of the paintings, estimates of their worth and legal considerations. After hours of discussions with lawyers, the traffickers in prison and Pablo's workers, a spreadsheet containing the assets was sent to the godfathers.

In Cali, Maria Victoria met the godfathers again. They scrutinised the spreadsheet, asset by asset. In the end, they announced that the debt could be paid in its entirety: half of it coming from Pablo's assets that the attorney general's office had seized, and the rest coming from assets that were not tied up in the court system. As Pablo's family would never have been granted the assets seized by the state, it was a relief that the godfathers could use their influence to obtain those assets.

The Castaño brothers ended up with acres of land and premium real estate. Fidel Castaño was an art dealer who owned dozens of Botero paintings. His artist connections included Salvador Dalí. A year after the settlement with Maria Victoria, Fidel went missing, presumed dead. The DEA stated in 2004 that they thought Fidel was working as an art dealer in Europe and

Israel, but, in September 2013, his remains were found in a mass grave in Colombia.

At the meeting, Carlos Castaño told Maria Victoria that he had Pablo's Dali painting, *Rock and Roll*, worth $3 million. He offered to return it, so that she could use it to pay the godfathers. As a gesture of good will, she told him to keep it, and that she would forward the title to him. Other creditors received art until Pablo's collection was diminished. They also received planes, helicopters, cars, motorbikes, jet-skis… After three hours, Miguel said that no one as monstrous as Pablo Escobar would ever be born in Colombia again. He praised Maria Victoria for getting in the good graces of Carlos Castaño by giving him the Dali painting.

At the next meeting, there were fewer creditors as many were satisfied with the assets they had received. Although the distribution of the assets had gone well, Gilberto was still insisting on killing Juan Pablo. Maria Victoria swore that Juan Pablo would never cause them any problems, and she would vouch for that with her life. The godfathers asked her to bring Juan Pablo to the next meeting.

Upon hearing that he was expected in Cali, Juan Pablo contemplated fleeing the country rather than end up in the hands of Los Pepes. Realising that leaving would put his mother's and sister's lives on the line, he knew that the meeting was unavoidable. Besides, where in the world could he hide from Los Pepes? The Castaños would enjoy hunting him to the ends of the earth to chop him into little pieces. If he didn't meet them, shake their hands and look in their eyes, they would assume he was forming an army somewhere to continue the war. Since his birth, Juan Pablo had been on the run from his father's enemies; with Pablo gone, he had inherited them. He couldn't understand why they felt so threatened by a teenager that they wanted him dead. Even if they killed him, he had to go to the meeting to protect his family.

Days of brooding convinced Juan Pablo that Gilberto would

order the death sentence. He wrote a will, leaving his few assets to his family and girlfriend. At night, he imagined Los Pepes torturing him in unimaginable ways to exact revenge for their family members who had suffered similar fates at the hands of Pablo's henchmen.

On the way to Cali, Juan Pablo and Maria Victoria discussed what to say at the meeting. At 6 pm, they arrived at a hotel and went to the eighth floor. To avoid getting poisoned, they didn't order any food and only drank tap water.

At 10 pm the next day, Pacho called. He wanted Maria Victoria to arrange a meeting with Pablo's side of the family to discuss the assets they had inherited. She told Pacho not to be concerned about that because Pablo had left a will, which the family would sort out. They were there to talk about peace with the godfathers, and for Juan Pablo to participate in the settlement.

At night, Juan Pablo cried and prayed. Whether he lived or died, it would all soon be over.

In the morning, a driver took them to the location's waiting room. They were surprised to see Pablo's mother and other relatives, with whom they'd fallen out as Juan Pablo and Maria Victoria were holding them accountable for cheating them out of money left to them by Pablo. They barely spoke to the other side of the family.

Eventually, a servant took them to a large room with couches, armchairs and a glass table. After they sat down, three of the godfathers came in excluding Gilberto. Then the family members from the waiting room entered. Miguel said they were there to discuss Pablo's inheritance. Pablo's mother and siblings had requested that the assets Pablo had left to his children should be included in the settlement. Pablo's mother said that certain buildings such as Monaco had been put in the children's names to prevent confiscation by the state. The assets belonged to Pablo, not the children, hence they should be included in the settlement.

Maria Victoria argued that Pablo had built those buildings for his children. That's why the rest of the assets had gone to other family members. She accused Pablo's mother of lying. Previously, the godfathers had warned Maria Victoria that the other side of the family was worthless and out to destroy her and her children. Pablo's mother's words at the meeting had backed up their claim. Miguel pointed out that he, too, had put assets in his children's names because he wanted his children to have them without any interference. The assets that Pablo had put in his children's names belonged to them. The rest should be divided up as Pablo's will instructed.

When the meeting about the assets was over, Juan Pablo and Maria Victoria followed the godfathers into another room. Sitting with their arms folded, the three godfathers scowled at Pablo's son.

Addressing them as gentlemen, Juan Pablo said that he had no reason to avenge his father's death. He wanted to get an education overseas, where he would not be a threat to anybody. However, being unable to leave the country, he could not pursue this plan. To stay alive, he knew he had to go.

Chepe warned him not to get involved in trafficking, para-military groups or anything of that nature. They did not want the resurrection of a second Pablo.

Juan Pablo said that one of his biggest life lessons was to learn that trafficking was a curse. Miguel took exception, citing his good life, his prosperous family, his properties and tennis courts, and that he walks daily... Juan Pablo apologised for offending Miguel. He said that trafficking had cost him everything: his father, family members, friends, peace, security and wealth. Such great losses had motivated him to avoid trafficking and any kind of trouble. Revenge wouldn't resurrect Pablo. He urged the god-fathers to help him to get overseas because no airline would sell him a ticket.

By the time Juan Pablo had finished, Miguel's demeanour had softened. He told Maria Victoria that her boy was going to get a second chance, but if he tried anything foolish then her life would be forfeited. He wanted her to promise that she would not allow him to go astray. In return, the children would get to keep the three buildings to support themselves financially as Pablo had intended in his will. Concerning the legal problems with the buildings and the government, Maria Victoria needed to contribute to a certain presidential candidate. The godfathers would then contact the new president, and remind him that she had given to his campaign.

Chepe told Juan Pablo not to worry. There was nothing to be afraid of. As long as Pablo's son did not attempt to become a trafficker, nothing bad would happen. They had called Juan Pablo to Cali to gauge whether he had good intentions. The only restriction they desired was that Juan Pablo be prevented from accessing too much money, which could tempt him to finance ideas about revenge.

Miguel advised them all not to worry any more. They could live safely in Cali if they wanted. Nobody would try to enact revenge for Pablo's deeds. He urged them to visit his wife's clothing store in Cali. He expressed optimism about the impending result of the presidential election, after which the godfathers would be in a better position to help them. After saying goodbye, Miguel told their driver to take them by his wife's clothing store.

Leaving the meeting unencumbered by Gilberto's death sentence, Juan Pablo felt lighter, even though a hurricane of mixed emotions battered his brain. The exuberance of having his life spared was tainted by the reality of seeing the other side of the family try to divest him of his inheritance. People he thought were his friends had converted into enemies and vice versa. He even felt thankful towards Los Pepes for not killing them.

When the driver stopped, Maria Victoria entered Miguel's wife's clothing store. In a trance induced by an adrenaline high, Juan Pablo opted to go into a men's clothing store nearby, where he bought a white bathrobe. He couldn't shake the thought that his head had been in a lion's mouth, only to emerge without a scrape.

Back in Bogotá, the excitement of the day wore off, and a

peaceful feeling enveloped the family, which they hadn't experienced in years. Their only outstanding concern was that even though the godfathers and Los Pepes were satisfied, there were still other dangerous creditors out there who might attempt something foolish. Nevertheless, with the main threat gone, they were in a celebratory mood, even though they were exhausted.

Carlos Castaño arranged for Maria Victoria to meet Don Berna – another of Pablo's associates who'd turned into an enemy – at a house in Medellín. Don Berna chastised her for marrying Pablo. Exasperated, Maria Victoria stated that she was a lady. She would not put up with any rudeness as she had earned the respect of the godfathers. The meeting ended with no progress.

Later on that night, Carlos Castaño called Maria Victoria. Don Berna was furious and capable of harming them. She needed to apologise and reach a settlement with him. At the next meeting with Don Berna, she apologised and gave him an apartment.

In the following weeks, Maria Victoria met many traffickers who presented endless demands and claims. Some tried to get her drunk to take advantage of her. Wise to their ways, she always refused the alcohol, which incensed them.

Carlos Castaño arranged for Maria Victoria to take a helicopter to negotiate a debt with Chaparro, a dangerous leader of a paramilitary group. Pablo had made thirteen attempts on his life and killed one of his sons. He'd survived a car bomb and a boat bomb. On the way, Carlos divulged information about Pablo's last day.

He said that Los Pepes had killed nearly all of Pablo's workforce and associates, but Pablo had remained so elusive that they were on the verge of quitting the hunt. Members of Los Pepes had started to resent the pressure from the Search Bloc's colonels to conclude the mission. Morale was down due to it being the end of the year. Many were going to leave by the end of December 1993. The eavesdropping technology provided by the US agencies wasn't good enough to pinpoint Pablo, so Los Pepes had obtained equipment from France.

The official story of the special forces killing Pablo was untrue. When it came to dangerous raids, the authorities always sent Los Pepes in first. While Carlos and his men raided Pablo's house, the troops had been waiting behind a shopping centre. Only after Pablo's death did they call them.

Upon hearing his door get hammered in, Pablo had fled upstairs barefoot. Los Pepes killed Pablo's bodyguard. Pursued, Pablo had shot back with his famous Sig Sauer pistol. Two shots had hit Carlos in his bullet-proof vest, knocking him over. Pablo rushed for a prearranged escape route through an open window and down a ladder, which took him onto the neighbour's roof. Men from Los Pepes were waiting on that side of the house. They shot Pablo in the shoulder and leg. Rushing after Pablo, Carlos had arrived at the window Pablo had climbed out of, only to see Pablo's corpse.

Maria Victoria asked Carlos to recover the bodies of five of her staff whom Los Pepes had slaughtered, including Manuela's nanny and a teacher. As they'd disposed of over 100 people, Carlos said it would be difficult to find the corpses.

After the helicopter landed in a field, Chaparro – backed up by 200 armed paramilitaries – greeted Carlos. He told Maria Victoria about Pablo's attempts on his life and the loss of his son. Maria Victoria said that she understood his situation, but she had no involvement in the war. She was just a mother who wanted to make peace.

Hours later, a settlement had been reached with Chaparro. He agreed to take 2,000 acres of land and a power plant at Nápolés. She said he could take anything he wanted from the Hacienda Nápolés estate – which the attorney general's office had seized – because she no longer considered it family property. Shaking her hand, he gave her permission to return to Hacienda Nápolés if she desired.

The godfathers sent a lawyer to Maria Victoria with a demand. She needed to contribute $50,000 to an amendment to legislation passing through Congress, which would guarantee the protection of traffickers' assets during confiscation hearings. Left with no choice, Maria Victoria borrowed the money.

In May 1994, demands were made by a trafficker, a middleman for the godfathers, who showed up at their apartment. He wanted Maria Victoria to make a generous contribution to Samper's presidential war chest. Numerous traffickers were doing so to get favourable treatment when it came to retrieving assets that had been seized by the state. Samper was also viewed as someone conducive to allowing Colombian citizens to seek sanctuary in foreign countries. Although short on cash, Maria Victoria managed to make payments by instalments. The benefits of these contributions proved elusive because no assets were suddenly freed by the government nor was any help forthcoming for them to safely exit the country.

Maria Victoria and Juan Pablo realised that the godfathers had bought the presidency. It was such a cosy relationship that the godfathers had an office on the same floor as the attorney general. Los Pepes frequented both offices. Anyone who wanted to discuss something with the godfathers would stop by the attorney general's office first. Attorney General de Greiff even joked about the godfathers' negotiations with Maria Victoria.

In August 1994, with Chaparro guaranteeing their safety, Maria Victoria, Juan Pablo and several family members went to Hacienda Nápolés, accompanied by three bodyguards provided by the state. Chaparro also sent men armed with AK-47s to protect them from guerrillas. They stayed in four cabins with bathrooms, but the air conditioning was only working in one. Driving around, they were disheartened by the dilapidation and the jungle having encroached upon the main house. They spotted hippos, submerged in the lakes, gazing at them. Over twenty years, Pablo's original four hippos had multiplied to thirty-five – creating the biggest wild hippo herd outside Africa – because their natural predators were absent in northern Colombia. The authorities had castrated four of them to try to slow their rate of reproduction. They showed up in villages, where the locals treated them as pets.

In late 1994, the godfathers requested a meeting with Maria Victoria and Juan Pablo to resolve outstanding issues with a helicopter and airplane that had belonged to Pablo. All of their assets were gone, except for the three buildings left to his children. Thirty people were present in Cali, most of whom had attended the first meetings.

As the meeting drew to a close, Miguel asked Maria Victoria why she hadn't approached the godfathers earlier when the war could have been avoided. She said she had wanted to, but Pablo would not listen to her. She had sent overtures through a Cali bodyguard who was a distant family member. The godfathers had responded positively, so she had told Pablo that in seeking peace for their children she had arranged a meeting. Pablo had insisted that such a meeting would only happen over his dead body. He called her crazy and naïve. He said that she would have been murdered in Cali and wrapped in barbed wire.

Maria Victoria applied for entry into various countries, but was denied. She tried to get help from the Catholic Church, the United Nations, the International Committee of the Red Cross, Colombian ex-president Turbay and even a recent recipient of the Nobel Peace Prize, but none were amenable. Turbay reminded her that Pablo had kidnapped his daughter, who had died slowly from a gunshot wound in the back after a rescue attempt.

Hoping to have better luck if they changed their names, they petitioned Attorney General de Greiff. He was reluctant until Maria Victoria threatened to go public with her knowledge of his dealings with the Cali Cartel and Los Pepes. In early 1994, they received new identities and de Greiff even introduced them to someone purporting to be an African countess connected to the president of Mozambique. For the right price, the African country would accept them as a humanitarian gesture. Jewellery and works of art were acceptable payment.

In December 1994, the family flew via Buenos Aires, which they particularly enjoyed. Then onto South Africa and Mozambique. The plan was to spend ten years in Africa, but the war-torn country repulsed them so much that they only lasted three days. As they'd liked Argentina so much, they settled there. For several years, they lived anonymously. Juan Pablo studied computing and industrial design. Maria Victoria invested in real estate through an accountant, who embezzled her. In order to keep their money, he leaked their real names. The media went wild and they were all arrested. The children were released, but Maria Victoria remained incarcerated on bogus money-laundering allegations.

She issued a statement: "I am a prisoner in Argentina for being Colombian. They want to try the ghost of Pablo Escobar because they want to prove that Argentina is combatting drug trafficking."

After a Nobel Peace Prize winner petitioned the court, she was released. Despite all of the interest in Pablo, she lived a quiet life away from the media.

A decade later, they were asked to participate in a 2009 Argentine-Colombian documentary film called *Sins of My Father*. Their initial reluctance was overcome by assurances that the film promoted reconciliation, that it did not glamorise Pablo's lifestyle and that Pablo's daughter would be excluded. Juan Pablo was filmed in Colombia meeting the sons of some of his father's political victims.

CHAPTER 8
THE DEA AND COLONEL
VELAZQUEZ

The Cali Cartel's role in eliminating Pablo generated goodwill from the public and the government, who were exasperated by all of the bombings and assassinations. The godfathers tried to capitalise on the goodwill by entering surrender negotiations with Gustavo de Greiff. Considered to be more sympathetic to their cause than the president, the old pipe-smoking Attorney General de Greiff was a former academic who had visited Pablo's family to hear their concerns about Los Pepes.

The godfathers offered to quit the cocaine business and serve time if de Greiff could guarantee them immunity from prosecution. With Pablo gone, the godfathers were no longer worried about getting assassinated in prison by Pablo's hit men. But during negotiations, de Greiff proved to be a stickler. After one meeting, Miguel left shaking his head and remarked that it was impossible to bribe a man who drove an old Volkswagen.

Not wanting to end up with the US sending special forces after them, the godfathers made overtures to the Clinton administration. At a restaurant, the cartel's head of its legal committee and its security head, Jorge, met an FBI agent. The godfathers hoped that by financing Los Pepes their alliance with the American agencies, especially the CIA, had been strengthened. Having all worked together to get rid of Pablo, surely the godfathers would now be allowed to retire peacefully with their assets intact. At the meeting, the cartel lawyer gave the usual spiel about the godfathers being legitimate businessmen with investments in various enterprises, including pharmacies, office and apartment buildings, banks, car dealerships, radio stations and soccer teams. Due to the war with Pablo, they had been illegitimately portrayed as traffickers. The FBI agent left unimpressed and never contacted the Cali Cartel, which the godfathers failed to perceive as ominous.

With the Cold War having thawed, the interests profiting from the US military needed new enemies to justify spending billions of taxpayers' money. With Pablo gone, the Cali Cartel was an ideal target. Aware of the negotiations with de Greiff and fearful that the godfathers could strike a deal at any time, the US directed its resources towards the Cali Cartel, but not the Castaño brothers, who had also taken over some of Pablo's cocaine infrastructure. Fighting left-wing guerrillas allied the Castaños with the interests of the Colombian government, the US government, the CIA and corporations. They received official protection and were allowed to traffic cocaine.

Out of all the people working for the Cali Cartel, one of the first to realise the American government's intentions was Jorge. The godfathers had hired the ex-army officer to protect their families during the war with Pablo. After five years of working for the cartel, he knew that the Americans were coming for them. He yearned to get out of the way and start his own security company.

As the war with Pablo was over, Jorge politely told Miguel that his work was done and he wanted to resign. Scowling, the godfather barked that quitting was unacceptable. Jorge was family now and Miguel needed him. Things were going to improve and Miguel had new opportunities for him. His boss's temperament frightened Jorge. As the head of security, he knew so much that if the godfathers viewed him as a liability they could easily order his disappearance. Feigning renewed interest in staying employed, he thanked Miguel for the opportunities and his confidence in him. With no way out, Jorge departed feeling trapped in a nightmare. He pledged to bide his time and come up with a way to escape from what he now viewed as a corrupt entity.

Things looked better for Jorge as the negotiations with the attorney general improved. If the godfathers surrendered, then his services would no longer be required. To announce the good news about de Greiff, the godfathers arranged a meeting with their senior staff at a dairy farm owned by Pacho. Over 100 bosses and lieutenants were served steaks and seafood, which they ate out of Styrofoam and cardboard using their cars as tables.

Gilberto climbed onto a table to address the crowd. Everyone hushed. Enthusiastically, he announced that there had been progress with de Greiff. They were going to be allowed to keep their assets, their real estate and their business interests outside of cocaine. They had six months to retire their cocaine labs and quit trafficking. They all had to comply or else the deal was off.

Abruptly, the mood in the room changed. Miguel was due to speak, but dissenters started to yell. Many of them had no criminal record, so they didn't want to turn themselves in and admit to crimes when they were making more money than ever now that Pablo was gone. One said he couldn't possibly quit in six months because he had just bought a plane. How could they untangle their financial responsibilities in such a short period? They had bills to pay and families to take care of. They had invested large sums of money. They were awaiting payments on big shipments...

After checking the security of the building, Jorge had positioned himself at the back of the crowd. The announcement about de Greiff had raised his spirits, but the revolt was unsettling him. He overheard someone say that the godfathers were rich enough to retire, but the senior staff could not afford to.

Unable to restore calm, Miguel yelled that they would be foolish not to accept the once-in-a-lifetime deal. The crowd roared back that six months wasn't enough. They needed at least a year or more. The godfathers needed to negotiate better conditions. With Miguel still on top of the table, many of the traffickers turned their backs towards him and left the building. If they had done that individually, they would have ended up dead. Their solidarity taunted the godfathers.

The meeting had gone so badly that the godfathers fell back on hoping to use their wealth to bribe key members of the government, the police and the military. If the deal with de Greiff was off, then surely the methods that had worked in the past would guarantee their safety.

The special forces that had helped to hunt down Pablo had been headquartered in Medellín, but the Colombian government relocated their headquarters to Cali. This was a clear indication that, with Pablo gone, the godfathers had been designated as the primary target in the War on Drugs by the America government – now run by Bill Clinton.

In September 1994, the DEA unsealed indictments against two Cali Cartel transportation directors. For two years, the DEA had been monitoring cocaine shipment routes from Colombia through Mexico into a hub at Los Angeles and onto other distribution points throughout America. The DEA was employing the Kingpin Strategy, which had been designed to attack the traffickers at their most vulnerable areas: the chemicals needed to process the drugs, their finances, transportation, communications and leadership infrastructure in the US. Run from the DEA's headquarters, the Kingpin Strategy advocated the selection of a finite number of targets for intensive investigative activity.

Claiming a victory in the War on Drugs, the DEA boasted that over two years they had arrested 166 alleged members of the Cali Cartel's distribution network and seized over six tons of cocaine and $13 million. The surveillance techniques used had included tapping cell phones and training state highway patrol officers to recognise smugglers.

"It is unequivocally clear that the cartels control every aspect of the cocaine trade, from the amount of cocaine to be shipped on consignment, right down to the markings on each package," the DEA said.

The probe had also exposed the latest methods of smuggling by the Cali Cartel. Some of the packages seized had been stamped with the president's name. Perhaps an inside joke on Bill Clinton's cocaine abuse – so severe that he had to be treated for sinus problems – and his half-brother Roger Clinton's arrest for dealing cocaine in 1985. Some packages had been covered in grease and coffee in the hope of thwarting drug-sniffing dogs. To transport cocaine, the cartel had used commercial and private planes, trucks, cars and increasingly boats because only a fraction of container ships could possibly be inspected.

The compartmentalised nature of the Cali Cartel was problematic for the DEA. Having made 200 arrests, little useful information was forthcoming because the arrestees did not know their employers' names. The Medellín Cartel had never been so compartmentalised. Pablo used to send large shipments by air and seek cash-and-carry customers, whereas the Cali Cartel restricted cocaine shipments to those already consigned for.

The DEA admitted making mistakes. In 1993, a major suspect realised he was being tailed. After leading them down a dead-end road, he asked his pursuers why they were following him.

"We're just out here in the neighbourhood. We're not following you," an agent said.

The DEA promptly intercepted a call, during which the suspect told his staff to close operations.

"We had to take him because we didn't want him out of the US, where he wouldn't answer to the justice system," the DEA said. "Most of these are a dead-end. You take down a cell or a couple of cells, and you're usually not going to find where it picks back up."

The DEA knew that the distribution systems it had intercepted would be replaced, while hoping there would be a high cost to the Cali Cartel in time and money. It aimed to hurt the cartel by arresting its more experienced members, whose jobs were harder to fill.

A method of transporting cocaine unknown to the DEA was in canisters of chlorine gas. Colombia imported this poisonous substance for industrial purposes, and the empty canisters were exported to America to be refilled. Such transfers were routine, so customs officials paid little attention. Besides, who would want to open and inspect anything so toxic? Due to its legitimate business interests, the cartel could easily order numerous quantities of the canisters. The problem was disposing of the gas.

In January 1994, four cartel employees assigned to dispose of the gas were experimenting with a new method. They lifted a sewage-system manhole lid and dropped in a hosepipe attached to a chlorine-gas tank on a truck. Assuming that the hosepipe was deep enough, one of the workers twisted a valve and the gas escaped into the hose. No leaks were detected from the hose, but lime-green gas started to rise from the manhole. As the gas assaulted their throats, the men feared for their lives and fled to the truck. After the gas was turned off, the truck departed. At a safe distance, they stopped to reel in the hose.

As they left the scene, the gas spread through the sewage system and into people's houses. Startled awake, people began to choke and gasp and wince all over the neighbourhood. Cries for help escalated into a general panic. Emergency responders smashed doors down to extract victims. People staggered around, choking and vomiting. Three children died. People were hospitalised by any means of transportation available, including taxis. The Red Cross established an emergency centre and the neighbourhood was classified as a disaster zone. Over 400 were injured. Out of the dozens hospitalised with lung burns, some died in the following months. The media called it an industrial accident. Nobody was held to account.

By March 1994, the Search Bloc had relocated its headquarters to Cali, where the American government lavished the troops with weapons, technology and accessories. Just like with the takedown of Pablo, weapons manufacturers were raking in millions at the US taxpayer's expense. A major invited Jorge to watch and photograph the arrival of the equipment, so that the cartel knew what they were up against. Jorge was allowed to inspect a spy plane stored by the CIA in a secure hangar. With the spy plane designed to monitor cartel operations at night, Jorge devised operational changes that would thwart the surveillance. He requested to be notified when the spy plane was airborne.

During 1993, the previous boss of the Search Bloc in Cali hadn't launched a single raid. Perhaps his meetings with the godfather Miguel had kept him too busy. The new Search Bloc boss, Colonel Velazquez, was determined to become the cartel's nemesis. Immune to bribery, he sought military glory and coveted becoming a general. He was a stickler for procedure, which annoyed his underlings, whose views of him ranged from having no common sense to being pompous and arrogant. Fortunately for the cartel, the aide to the previous Search Bloc boss carried his position over to Colonel Velazquez. Code-named Ernesto by the godfathers, the aide was on the cartel's payroll.

The cartel sent a politician to Colonel Velazquez in the hope of gauging his attitude towards the godfathers. They met at a restaurant. After dessert was served, the politician said, "Unlike Pablo Escobar, the Rodríguez Orejuela family are not bad people. They are interested in meeting with you, and for your time and friendship, they would like to compensate you with around $300,000."

The colonel stood, scowled in disgust at the politician and stormed out of the restaurant. Ernesto notified the cartel that when the colonel had returned to the headquarters he had reported the attempted bribery by the politician to his bosses and the US government.

The closest homes to the Search Bloc's headquarters were filled with people loyal to the cartel, such as the family members of cartel bodyguards. Their job was to monitor the headquarters, especially who was going in and out, and to immediately report when a convoy left for a raid. Some of the lookouts were assigned to follow the convoys, and keep the cartel updated by radio.

The colonel's phone was tapped. A transmitter inside his computer relayed conversations in its vicinity back to the cartel. The cartel set up an electronic surveillance post on a hill opposite the colonel's office, which provided a bird's-eye view of the headquarters. The experts the colonel hired to remove bugging devices were the same people who had installed the devices for the cartel.

The colonel hosted two CIA agents, who lived in the garrison. The agents ordered cable television. Cartel engineers put a transmitter in their cable box. The CIA installed a bug in Miguel's sister's offices. Tipped off by the colonel's boss, General Zuniga, Miguel learned that the bug was inside a strip of wood. It was promptly destroyed.

The colonel received a call, describing packages getting unloaded at the Cali airport. In charge of a convoy, he raced off to seize the contraband. Having intercepted the call, the cartel notified its workers on the scene, who were on a smoke break, having unloaded millions in cash from a Boeing 727. A dump truck full of cash trundled out of the airport as the special forces arrived.

Conversations intercepted by the cartel showed a romance developing between the colonel and a high-class female informant. This interested the godfathers because the colonel was married. On a regular basis, the colonel started to meet the lady for dinner.

On a call to the colonel, the lady reported that she was aware of a cluster of armed bodyguards at a medical building, guarding someone of great importance. Getting treatment for a skin condition, the godfather Pacho was alerted and abandoned the building.

Hoping to capitalise on photos of the colonel romancing the lady, Miguel set about finding her identity by contacting the colonel's aide. Ernesto identified her as Dolly, the beautiful and cantankerous ex-wife of a rancher in her late thirties. Upon finding her husband swimming with naked women, she'd once driven a car into the pool. Godfather Chepe met Dolly. For a price, she agreed to a blackmail scheme.

Having once been Dolly's neighbour, Jorge was assigned to run the program. Meeting at a hotel restaurant, vivacious Dolly turned her charm on Jorge. Over breakfast, Dolly said that she was a single mother with a teenage daughter. Using government money, the colonel was paying her $250 a week, which she needed.

When asked about sex with the colonel, Dolly admitted that they had sometimes gone to a bar and a motel. He was always in the mood. She had to put up resistance otherwise they would have ended up in a motel every night. Jorge said that he wanted to film the next rendezvous. Taken aback, Dolly paused, but finally relented.

At 10 pm on a Monday, the couple arrived at the colonel's preferred bar. In a booth, they kissed and cuddled. At a table taking photos, Jorge was with a female radio dispatcher, who was pretending to be his partner. The positioning of the tables had been arranged by a bar manager, who had turned the volume of the music up to disguise the clicking of Jorge's camera.

With the colonel eager to leave, Dolly consented. They took a short drive. The motel's marquee included the apple from the Garden of Eden and a serpent. The motel was owned by a trafficker friend of Miguel's, who had allowed the cartel full access. The colonel parked in a garage. A concierge escorted them to a suite with a minibar, free pornography and a camera hidden on an air-conditioning duct. In an adjacent room, Jorge started the video camera, which was aimed at the king-size bed. The overenthusiastic colonel got down to business. Before an hour was up, the couple checked out.

Watching the video the next day, the exuberant godfathers acted like teenage boys, commenting and joking about the colonel's bedroom manners. The consensus was that the colonel was a selfish lover who lacked staying power. Copies of the tape were made, including a version edited down to just over ten minutes.

Ernesto revealed that the colonel was going to raid the wedding party for Gilberto's daughter Claudia. On the scheduled day, May 14, 1994, Gilberto convened the godfathers. They all contributed towards a letter to the colonel, which Gilberto typed up. It mocked the colonel's sexual ability and suggested that he mind his own business.

Accompanied by a sex tape and photos from the bar, the letter was sent to the colonel at 10 am. A retired army captain who worked for the cartel delivered it. He said that he'd been forced by two armed men on motorbikes to take the package.

The colonel shook his head and took the package into his office. Two hours later, his aide notified the cartel that the colonel had not left his room, which was full of cigarette smoke. After mulling over his predicament for a few hours, the colonel chose not to be cowed. He reported the blackmail attempt and confessed to having improper relations with an informant.

In a vengeful mood, the colonel set about coordinating the raid on Gilberto's daughter's wedding. He boasted to his aide that the Chess Player was going to get a big surprise when the colonel arrested him at the celebration. A Search Bloc convoy set off at dusk, heading for a party expected to attract hundreds of guests. They were followed by lookouts on motorbikes, who reported the convoy's every move to the cartel.

Wearing tuxedos, Gilberto and his brothers were sitting on a patio sipping whiskey, receiving updates from Jorge about the location of the special forces.

The troops arrived at the location designated for the wedding. Armed with rifles, they raided a party of over 400 people. The trapped women screamed. The colonel's men demanded to know where Gilberto was.

Far away from the raid, Gilberto and his family were at a safe location. The wedding had been switched to a village and only family and close friends had attended. As the wedding drew to a close, Gilberto joked about having a last dance with his daughter. Not wanting to risk extending the great celebration they'd had, Miguel ushered the brothers home.

CHAPTER 9
KEY PLAYERS FALLING

With the authorities applying increased pressure, the godfathers needed a strategy that would render them untouchable. They decided to put in power the top man in the country. It cost over $6 million to install Ernesto Samper as the president of Colombia. After his victory was announced, Miguel banged his fist on a desk in a celebratory way and yelled that they'd bought a president. Assuming that investigations into the cartel would be dropped, the godfathers were ecstatic.

Having transferred resources to Cali to apprehend the godfathers, the DEA was disheartened by Samper's victory. It decided to fight back by attempting to topple the president. It wanted Samper replaced by someone more devoted to the War on Drugs. The DEA leaked a recording of a phone call in which Miguel talked about donating over $2 million to the presidential campaign. The scandal culminated with the US government threatening to stop financial aid to Colombia, and the presidential rival demanding a re-election.

The godfathers penned a letter disavowing any contributions. Initially, Samper denied taking hot money. Then his aides admitted accepting it on his behalf. As Samper's own Liberal Party was in charge of the congressional hearings investigating the scandal, he managed to cling onto the presidency.

Even though Samper had not been toppled, the scandal worked in the DEA's favour. Hoping to restore his credibility, Samper pledged to go after the traffickers. The DEA waited to see if Samper would follow through or whether his pledge was the usual hyperbole.

In July 1994, the cartel intercepted information that indicated a raid was imminent on the offices of its head accountant, Pallomari, a bespectacled clean-shaven man in a business suit. When notified, Pallomari said there was nothing to worry about because all of his records were in order and the businesses were legitimate. The following day, the lookouts living outside the Search Bloc's headquarters radioed reports of a raid party emerging. On motorbikes, some of the lookouts followed the convoy as it weaved towards Pallomari's office. As if in a dream world, Pallomari did not order the evacuation of his offices or the removal of the vast amounts of files pertaining to the godfather's money-laundering and investments. Even worse, he stayed for the raid. The special forces arrested him, and seized the documents.

While the godfathers arranged to get Pallomari released on bail, he was talking to the authorities. He admitted working for Gilberto and Miguel. Having expected him to keep their names out of it, Gilberto was furious. He said that the authorities had to hit Pallomari to get him to talk, but they also had to hit him again to get him to shut up because he had so much to say. Gilberto wanted him disposed of, but Miguel intervened and promised to keep Pallomari out of sight.

After getting released, Pallomari realised that he had put his own life on the line, and that of his wife and two boys. He signed legal papers stating that he did not work for the godfathers. Instead of returning to resume his interview with the authorities, he hid.

The documents provided the colonel whom the godfathers had tried to blackmail a victory against the cartel, which he had been craving ever since watching the sex tape. Colonel Velazquez promptly ordered more raids on addresses found in the documents. A raid on Pallomari's data centre revealed meticulous records of bribes. Hundreds of police on the cartel's payroll were fired. The colonel's success made it appear as if the president was honouring his pledge by clamping down on the Cali Cartel.

In 1994, the godfathers took hits on multiple fronts. Having expanded into the Florida cocaine market since the demise of Pablo, the cartel suffered the arrest of four of its five Miami bosses. Unknown to the godfathers, the Miami bosses were cutting deals to avoid lengthy sentences. The disintegration of the Florida operation meant shifting more drugs through Mexico. As the authorities delved further into the records seized from Pallomari, more cartel workers and informants were exposed.

The scandal with the presidential contributions was still taking its toll. The Clinton administration was unhappy with President Samper. America bent Colombia to its will through billions in foreign aid, which the US was threatening to withhold. The US State Department denied visas to Colombian officials. The CIA director refused to meet his Colombian counterparts.

A federal wiretap caught Miguel coordinating a one-ton shipment of cocaine with an employee in the US. The evidence resulted in indictments against Miguel and Gilberto in America and Colombia. The godfathers hired lawyers in both countries. Two witnesses serving time in prison were flown from America to Colombia to testify against the godfathers. The witnesses received $50,000 to keep quiet on the stand, and the charges were dismissed in Colombia. Others arrested in America were released on bail posted by the cartel. They resumed work in Colombia or other countries involved in cartel operations.

The goodwill that the Cali Cartel had earned by working with the CIA and Los Pepes to kill Pablo was gone, but the godfathers were suffering the complacency associated with getting away with crimes for too long and being able to bribe all levels of government. They still believed that they could broker a better deal with the Colombian government than the one Pablo had negotiated for his imprisonment in the Cathedral. Their expectations ranged from house arrest to an amnesty for their crimes that included no prison time.

The vast War on Drugs' resources were now pitted against the cartel. US pressure forced the Colombian president to drop the

National Police chief, and to replace him with someone amenable to US interests. The new chief, General Serrano, fired approximately 2,000 of his underlings whom he suspected of corruption.

Attorney General de Greiff lost his job, which went to a cousin of the presidential candidate, Galán, whose assassination had been blamed on Pablo. The former prosecutor announced that no deal would be cut for the godfathers. He granted numerous warrants to General Serrano to launch raids on cartel interests. Rewards of over $1 million were offered for information leading to the capture of the godfathers. President Samper added 1,600 people to a joint army-police unit fighting drug trafficking.

At a meeting with the godfathers, Jorge aired his concerns about the threat from America. With General Noriega in a US federal prison and Pablo Escobar gone, the godfathers were now the faces of the main enemy in the War on Drugs. Gilberto thanked Jorge, but Miguel was dismissive. He reduced Jorge's security responsibilities by handing some of them over to his son, William, who put his friend Dario, an ex-army lieutenant, in charge.

In 1995, President Clinton threatened to pull vast amounts of aid by striking off Colombia as a partner in the War on Drugs. The US Assistant Secretary of State for International Narcotics Matters told the Colombian president that further aid was dependent upon the arrest of the Cali Cartel leaders. With so much money at risk, President Samper sent a former senator to notify the godfathers that he could not help them anymore because his hands were tied. He said their best strategy was to avoid getting caught.

An investigation into the cartel by the DEA was producing results. Operation Cornerstone had begun in 1991 with the seizure of 12,000 kilos of cocaine disguised with concrete fence posts. In April 1991, the authorities apprehended Harold Ackerman, one of the first powerful managers to cooperate against the cartel. His importance was such that he was nicknamed the Cali Cartel's ambassador to the United States. As a

Colombian citizen, Ackerman had studied industrial engineering and business administration at a university in Cali. After graduating, he had worked at a clothing manufacturer. In June 1981, he had moved to America and started a dress shop in Dadeland Mall, Miami.

Colombians at Ackerman's business said that he could enjoy riches beyond his wildest dreams by working for an organisation based in Cali. As he enjoyed spending money, he joined the cartel. In October 1991, he helped to facilitate the importation of 5,000 kilos of cocaine hidden in frozen broccoli. He was paid $120,000 for the first shipment, $200,000 for the second and $400,000 for the third. Over two years, he made $3 million.

On April 23, 1991, his North Miami home was raided. The authorities found jewellery worth $200,000, a safe containing $462,000 in cash and five expensive cars. At first, Ackerman refused to talk. If he opened his mouth, his family members in Colombia would suffer the consequences.

Miguel sent a message via a lawyer: "Don't be concerned, Harold. Take it easy. Your family will receive a monthly payment." The lawyer added, "[Miguel] told me to remind you that as a friend he is a very good person, but as an enemy, he will be a very bad person. Think of cooperating and not even your dog will remain. Remember, you still have family in Colombia."

Facing six life sentences, Ackerman contemplated cooperating as a way out. After the DEA guaranteed his family's protection, he agreed to testify. On the stand, the businessman was so articulate that he became known as one of the most important witnesses ever. He detailed the cartel's structure, methods and smuggling routes. He exposed the US lawyers who were working for the benefit of the cartel. "My cooperation with the United States," Ackerman testified, "provided a detailed, minute and true narration of my activities in narcotics smuggling. I was involved with the Rodriguez Orejuela organisation."

After learning about Ackerman's cooperation, Miguel became ill. The godfathers convened a series of crisis-management meetings. To keep everything running smoothly required massive amounts of cash, but all of the arrests were draining the cartel's liquidity.

Other co-defendants in Operation Cornerstone included prominent American lawyers who had served as attorneys for the cartel in the US, including a former chief of the Office of International Affairs at the Department of Justice, two former Assistant US attorneys and 56 others. The indictment alleged that they had participated in offering, arranging and delivering monthly subsistence payments to the family members of traffickers arrested as part of Operation Cornerstone and related investigations. In addition to the subsistence payments, the godfathers had paid their legal fees in exchange for the defendants keeping quiet about the cartel. The indictment charged that many of the lawyers laundered drugs' proceeds on behalf of the cartel. By their actions, the lawyers inhibited efforts by law enforcement to neutralise the cartel's trafficking activities, and enabled the cartel to continue its operations. In June 1995, the final phase of Operation Cornerstone resulted in the indictment of 61 cartel members.

The proliferation of arrests necessitated millions in legal fees and bribes. Attempting to micromanage an expanding set of problems increased Miguel's stress and health issues. Suffering from hypoglycaemia and migraine headaches, he often felt weak and faint. Not known for possessing a good temper, he was even more abrupt with his underlings.

With the Pallomari records causing so much damage to the cartel, the godfathers feared that his capture and extradition to America would compound the disaster. If Pallomari's life ended, then so would the liability. With his work so invaluable, he couldn't be assassinated until a replacement was found. Pallomari's tasks were slowly given to Miguel's son, William, who, unlike Gilberto's children, was being groomed to run the cartel in the event of the godfathers' arrests. Sensing his fate, Pallomari went underground, knowing full well that it was only a matter of time before the cartel found him.

CHAPTER 10
THE DEA AGENTS

According to the Colombian media, there were hundreds of DEA agents in Cali hunting down the godfathers. In reality, there were only four agents gathering intelligence on the Cali Cartel for the DEA's Group One Task Force in Bogotá. For security purposes, they generally worked in pairs. The younger pair was Chris Feistl and Dave Mitchell. Both in their early 30s, and over six-feet tall and blonde, they looked more like Beastie Boys fans than narcotics agents. Chris was formerly a policeman in Virginia Beach, whereas Dave had been in an airborne infantry division of the US Army, which specialised in parachute assaults. Having joined the DEA in 1988, they knew each other from operations in Miami.

The other pair had nicknamed themselves Batman and Robin. They spoke Spanish and blended into Colombia far more easily than the blonde giants. The Palestinian-American Jerry Salameh spoke softly and exuded warmth in contrast to his partner, Ruben Prieto, a heavyset Mexican-American boxing and martial arts expert with an immovable face and an outspoken nature.

The partners alternated their shifts. Such dangerous work required that they stayed in at night and kept low profiles in the day. They developed informants, but when the leads were followed up, the godfathers always remained elusive. By gathering intelligence, the agents learned that the godfathers' preferred method of escaping from the police was not to engage in shootouts, but to disappear into the walls of luxury properties spread out across Cali. The safe houses had been fitted with caletas, carefully constructed compartments with reinforced walls in elaborate hiding places, equipped with oxygen supplies and everything necessary to enable the godfathers to remain entombed for long durations.

Some had been designed with the same dimensions as coffins. Getting into a compartment was easy, but once it was locked from the inside, it was inaccessible. If it was located, tools and equipment were required to break it open. The compartments were so hard to identify that the authorities rarely needed tools.

With so many locals on the cartel's payroll, the DEA's strategy was to offer huge sums of money to anyone who could provide information that led to the whereabouts and arrest of the godfathers. In a country where many were toiling for a pittance, the DEA believed that some would risk their lives for rewards of up to $2 million. To advertise the rewards and to put pressure on the godfathers, wanted leaflets were dropped on Cali. The US government financed TV commercials produced by the Colombian government, offering millions of dollars for information leading to the arrest of the godfathers. As the godfathers had infiltrated the telephone company, they obtained the phone records of the people who had contacted the hotline to provide information. The informants started to disappear. Over six weeks, 75 corpses were found with injuries associated with torture.

The most compelling information provided by the informants concerned Flaco, Gilberto's personal secretary: in his mid-30s and dressed sharply, Flaco could lead the agents to Gilberto. In May 1995, the Mexican-American agent Prieto was reading worldwide DEA reports when he spotted a reference to Flaco in Cali. The report was from the DEA's office in Quito, Ecuador, which Prieto contacted. He asked whether it was the same Flaco who reputedly worked for Gilberto. The agent didn't know, so he arranged a meeting with the source: an informant code-named Andy.

In Bogotá, Prieto met Andy, a financial expert who had laundered tens of millions. The DEA had learned about Andy in 1994 after agents had captured one of his couriers in New York. Busted in Ecuador by the DEA, Andy had been given a choice of switching sides or getting extradited to America.

At the Embassy Suites, Prieto told Andy, "We have information that to get to Gilberto Rodriguez Orejuela, we have to get to his right-hand man. And to get to him, we have to get to you. You know exactly why it's good for you to work with us. And I'm sure you are aware of the reward money being offered on TV."

Andy described Flaco as skinny and with an unusual walk: like a duck with his feet pointing outwards. Although he provided solid information, Andy had a crack cocaine habit. Prieto convinced Andy to go to Cali to track down Flaco within two days.

Two days went by and Prieto never heard from Andy, so he started to search Cali. The tough Mexican-American found Andy in an apartment frequented by gangsters. Leaving his DEA partner, Salameh, in an undercover car, Prieto climbed the stairs of the building and knocked on a door. Dressed only in underwear, Andy answered, his eyes bloodshot and wide from smoking crack. He yelled at Prieto for showing up unannounced. Flaco was scheduled to arrive at any moment, but Prieto's arrival would get them both killed. Undaunted, Prieto chastised Andy for not calling and leaving him waiting like an idiot. Doubting that Flaco would show up, Prieto asked what car he was driving. Andy said a red Mazda.

Sceptical but not wanting to jeopardise Andy's cover, Prieto departed. A skinny man ascended the stairs right by him, walking bowlegged. Simultaneously, they turned their heads to check each other out, both remaining poker-faced. In the undercover car, Prieto told Salameh that Flaco was inside. Excited by the breakthrough, they waited until Flaco emerged. They followed him to his residence. At a police base, the DEA organised a plan to keep tabs on Flaco.

Over a month, DEA agents and Colombian policemen trailed Flaco as he started out on his journey to Gilberto's hideout. Flaco made their job difficult by employing numerous counter-surveillance techniques. He altered his routes, walked in circles, jumped in taxis, entered and exited and re-entered buildings... Just when the team members thought they had figured out his methods and had prepared a plan to thwart them, they would put the plan into effect, and Flaco would lose them within minutes. Frustrated, they started to blame each other. Then they came up with a different plan.

Due to Flaco's hypervigilance, the team had to maintain a safe distance to remain undetected. Each day, the distance was reduced. A week later, they had covered his first five miles to Gilberto's hideout. Progress slowed when they kept losing track of him at Street 35 North.

The team recruited a group of Colombian policewomen, whom the CIA had trained. In plain clothes, they jogged up and down the stairs in a building that Flaco used as part of his disappearing act. Eventually, they spotted him walking bowlegged up the stairs, and taking a route along a street with five homes on a hill in the Santa Monica neighbourhood in the northern suburbs of Cali.

Prieto told the head of the National Police, General Serrano, that Flaco had led them to five townhouses, one of which contained Gilberto. Informants had indicated that Gilberto was about to be moved to a new hideout, and Prieto didn't want to start from scratch. He requested a quick raid to prevent the Chess Player from evading them. With little time for preparations, Serrano wanted to know what the chances were of catching Gilberto if a raid were launched immediately. Gazing hard at the general, Prieto stated that it was less than 50%, which was about as good as it would ever get for capturing Gilberto.

Prieto put forward a plan. If the Search Bloc were dispatched to the neighbourhood, Gilberto would be notified in advance. The best approach was to disguise troops in the covered truck that the general used as part of his armed backup. With the general scheduled to go to the airport to fly back to Bogotá, the escort could drive by the hill with the five homes. The troops could jump out of the back of the truck, and commence the hilltop raids with an element of surprise. A military helicopter could watch to ensure Gilberto didn't escape.

On the afternoon of June 9, the troops got inside the covered truck. Their leader was Colonel Barragan. The unit was considered the least corrupt. As the troops approached the hill, Prieto saw an old woman standing in a doorway of a house. He yelled at her to go inside for her own safety. She urged him to come and speak to her. When he arrived, she said in a hushed tone that she knew who he was looking for. In a hurry, he pressed her for an explanation. She said the people in the middle townhouse. Having lived there all of her life, she knew everybody in the neighbourhood except for the occupants of the middle townhouse who had only been there for less than two months. They kept their windows closed and never came outside. Delighted, Prieto urged the woman to go inside, so that the situation could be handled. He asked Colonel Barragan to send the troops to the middle townhouse.

The troops and the two DEA agents surrounded the white-stucco residence, while a helicopter circled. With the helicopter drawing nearer, the troops prepared to knock down the door. A young maid opened it, revealing Flaco and Gilberto's girlfriend. Surging with excitement, Prieto yelled that they were at the right place.

Pointing guns, the troops charged inside. Gilberto wasn't there. For an hour, the troops and the two DEA agents searched the rooms relentlessly. Upon achieving no result, the morale of the troops plummeted. Exhausted and believing they had wasted their time, they were on the verge of giving up.

With its options limited, the cartel tried to divert the troops by calling in a tip that the godfathers were meeting at another property in the vicinity, but the agents were not fooled.

On the second floor, Prieto was in the main bedroom, which had a large-screen TV against a wall. A fallen painting aroused his suspicion. A young thin soldier shoved the TV, but it didn't budge. An inkling that Gilberto had stashed himself behind it energised Prieto, who grabbed the TV. It moved, revealing a partially open door.

Inside the compartment, crouched on a floor covered with cash and holding a gun in each hand was Gilberto in his under-wear. Shaking, he pointed a gun at Prieto, who was unarmed and lacking a bullet-proof vest. The only equipment Prieto had was a camera around his neck. Gazing at Gilberto, who looked frightened enough to shoot him accidentally, Prieto froze.

Boots thudded into the room. Metal clicked as the troops trained their guns on Gilberto. Standing between Gilberto and the troops, Prieto swivelled his head to watch them fan out. He realised that if they fired at Gilberto, he would be killed.

"Please don't shoot. You won," Gilbert said, putting the guns down. "I surrender. Calm, boys. Don't kill me. I'm a man of peace." The troops approached and handcuffed the unshaven godfather.

While the Batman and Robin DEA agents enjoyed the glory, General Serrano was notified. Immediately, he changed direction from the Cali airport and headed towards the townhouse. In a helicopter, he escorted Gilberto to Bogotá, where armed police swarmed the godfather, whom they marched through the airport.

At the National Police's headquarters, a carnival atmosphere erupted in the main hall. The staff crowded balconies to observe the godfather, handcuffed, but impeccably dressed in trousers, a cream-colored windbreaker and a striped shirt. The police showered streamers and confetti down onto their commanders. Amid wild cheering, Gilberto was eventually exhibited to the media, appearing exhausted and bewildered. The fifty-six-year-old asked for his blood pressure to be checked by a doctor.

"When I heard the news [of Gilberto's arrest], I felt as if a piano had been lifted off my back," said President Samper, who had accepted over $6 million from the cartel. Samper went on national radio and TV to announce the news, which he said was "the beginning of the end for the Cali Cartel. We will not let up until this [drug] problem is completely eliminated from Colombia."

"This arrest should send a signal to other narco-traffickers that their insidious crimes will not be allowed to destroy the fabric of our people," said a White House spokesman on behalf of President Clinton, who, as Governor of Arkansas, had allowed the CIA to import cocaine through Mena, Arkansas, some of which had been obtained from the Medellín and Cali Cartels back when the cartels were contributing to the CIA's anti-Communist wars in South America.

"My hat is off to the Colombian Government and the Colombian people," said President Clinton's Drug Czar.

The DEA administrator announced: "This arrest is evidence that no drug Mafia leaders are above the law, no matter how powerful they are and no matter where they hide. The Government of Colombia is to be congratulated for their commitment and persistence. The arrest of Gilberto Rodriguez Orejuela signals the beginning of the end of the Cali Mafia... The Cali Mafia has spread its poison, death and destruction to the streets of small towns and major cities around the world.

"The United States and Colombia have worked closely together to target and capture these Cali Mafia leaders. Rodriguez Orejuela is a major kingpin in the world cocaine trade. Rodriguez Orejuela who is known as the 'Chess Player' has been backed into a corner. Thanks to the Colombian Government he has no moves left.

"General Serrano knew this day would come, and the United States is grateful for his commitment and bravery, and the commitment and bravery of the men and women of the Colombian National Police. I met with General Serrano a month ago and he personally assured me that he would do everything in his power to capture the kingpins. He has proven to be true to his word."

Pablo Escobar's death had taken "Medellín out of the picture and Cali supplanted them," a DEA official said. "But there is nobody around to supplant the [Cali] cartel." The DEA had no basis for these lies. It knew from alcohol prohibition that whenever a supplier was arrested, crime increased as others competed to take over the business; and supply, after a dip, always continued unabated. Traffickers across Colombia, including the Castaño brothers and Don Berna, were taking advantage of the huge profits in cocaine made possible by US drug laws and they were working with the CIA.

The *New York Times* reported that Gilberto was the most influential leader of the world's largest drug trafficking gang in Colombia and his arrest was the best news that US officials had had in years in the long-running battle against drugs.

The DEA announced that a 1989 US indictment for drug trafficking emanating in New Orleans and evidence shared with the Government of Colombia had provided the impetus for Gilberto's arrest. He was immediately indicted in Miami, along with other members of the cartel, for the illegal importation of over 200,000 kilos of cocaine over 10 years.

Although heralded as a victory in the War on Drugs, others knew that Gilberto's arrest would not impact the cocaine entering America, just like Pablo's hadn't.

"Just because the big boss disappears, the others don't disappear, neither do the economic interests, nor the problems the illegal business generates," said a professor of political science at the Javeriana University in Bogotá.

"I've always feared that when they capture or kill these big bosses, those that follow will be worse," said the head of the Colombian government's National Drugs Council.

Even the DEA conceded: "We still have a long way to go. Gilberto is certainly a prize, the leader with the most stature, but there are others out there and they're not going to quit."

"Besides, even though Gilberto was the main man," said a drug enforcement source, "his brother remains free and is capable of running things."

As Gilberto was considered to be the most moderate member of the cartel, some commentators feared that the more violent members would get increased power over the decision-making, and there would be a repeat of the explosion of violence associated with Pablo as the remaining Cali Cartel members felt increasingly threatened.

Bracing for retaliation by the cartel, the government dispatched soldiers to patrol the capital and more raids were launched in Cali. The day after Gilberto's arrest, a bomb exploded in downtown Medellín during a street festival, killing twenty-one and wounding 200. Traffickers claimed responsibility and cited Gilberto's arrest. The public worried about more attacks.

Gilberto's strategy was to avoid extradition to the US at all costs. Just like with his incarceration in Spain in 1984, his legal team set about discerning who to bribe to get a minimum sentence. Although he was facing a maximum of 24 years in Colombia if convicted, the likelihood of him playing the system did not go unnoticed. Under Colombian law, Gilberto could obtain a significant sentence reduction for good conduct and by gesturing cooperation.

"It's not just a question of capturing him, but of conducting a rigorous investigation," said a government ombudsman.

"He must get… the punishment he deserves," Bogotá's *El Tiempo* reported. "Nothing would be worse than to wipe out with one hand what was done with the other hand."

Gilberto denounced the charges and denied running the Cali Cartel, which he said the DEA had invented. He had a point: the word cartel was an invention of US prosecutors looking to provide structure to their indictments in complex cases and to obtain longer sentences.

His arrest motivated some key cartel workers to surrender in the hope of getting lesser sentences, rather than duking it out with the authorities and ending up like some of Pablo's men. Taking Gilberto alive instead of assassinating him had surprised many in the trafficking community. It showed that the government was willing to work with them instead of killing them on sight.

Ten days after Gilberto's arrest, the cartel's minister of war, the Scorpion, turned himself in. The Scorpion had once armed his men with chainsaws and ordered them to carve up 107 people who had expressed sympathy for trade unions. After a priest complained about the barbarity, his headless body was found in a river. On June 24, the leader of the cartel's hit men also surrendered.

With Gilberto inside, Miguel was in charge of running the cartel. The DEA agents Chris and Dave decided to employ the same method that had worked with Gilberto on capturing Miguel. They wanted the cartel workers who had been arrested in America as part of Operation Cornerstone questioned for information about Miguel. They wanted to know who was closest to Miguel. Which houses did he frequent? Who could be followed like Flaco to get him? Who else within the cartel would be willing to cooperate? What was the best arrest plan?

The agents received a ten-page letter from an Operation Cornerstone agent suggesting three candidates for tailing. One was Miguel's personal secretary, whom Chris and Dave already had under surveillance, but with no results. The second was a former Colombian government lawyer who worked for Miguel. Unenthused about the first two options, the agents were excited when they heard the third candidate: Jorge.

Having joined the cartel to protect people from Pablo, Jorge was increasingly unhappy with his new assignments from Miguel that involved tracking people down for cartel hit men. One job in particular provoked nightmares.

Celebrating his fifty-first birthday at home with family and friends, Miguel told Jorge that he was going to a ranch owned by Pacho that had a lake and a man-made beach. He wanted Jorge to interrogate a guest suspected of being involved in a cocaine shipment that had disappeared in Panama.

Anticipating finding the ranch full of partygoers, Jorge was surprised to encounter a throng of armed bodyguards. While making security checks, Jorge ran into the godfathers' most reliable hit man, Memo, who had thick dark hair and cold brown eyes. Memo asked Jorge what he was doing there. Jorge said he was waiting for the boss.

Two large cars parked. The Panamanian whom Jorge had been assigned to interrogate emerged and dashed to a bathroom. Armed bodyguards got out of the cars as well as an army major and a beautiful woman with short brown hair. The cars departed. Jorge drove around the perimeter of the ranch and went inside. In the presence of Pacho's animated bodyguards, the three Panamanians were despondent. The woman was alone on a couch, smoking. Jorge offered her a drink, but she declined.

A thudding sound, yelling and property getting destroyed drew Jorge down a corridor to a bedroom. He was disturbed to see the bodyguards attempting to pin down the major. With his military fitness, the major was resisting valiantly. Memo put a rope around the major's neck and skilfully used a piece of wood to tighten its grip. The major choked. His face turned purple. He defecated in his trousers, which stunk up the room. Maintaining a solemn expression to hide his shock, Jorge left the room.

Jorge found the Panamanian he was supposed to interrogate on a bathroom floor, trapped by armed guards. The Panamanian asked for Miguel. Jorge said that he didn't know what was going on, but he had a question from Miguel as to whether the Panamanian had anything to do with the DEA. The Panamanian insisted that there had been a big mistake. Even though he knew it was a lie, Jorge said that Miguel was on his way to continue the questioning.

The hit men roaming the ranch had switched from standby mode into animated killers. A specialist in disembowelling rushed past Jorge demanding a knife. Removing the bowels prevented corpses from surfacing when they had been thrown into a river.

Jorge found the beautiful woman who had arrived earlier sitting on a bed, smoking. Relieved she was still alive, he dreaded to imagine what was going to happen to her. Jorge went outside where three men were disposing of a body wrapped in blood-soaked curtains. They lifted the corpse and placed it in the back of a car, which took off for the river. When Jorge re-entered the ranch, it was unusually quiet. The killers had calmed down. The corpse of the woman was facing upwards, her lips freshly blue. The bruise around her neck suggested she had been strangled. Suddenly, her feet twitched and arched down. The specialist in disembowelling entered the room. Having no stomach for what was about to happen, Jorge left.

A few days later, Memo killed another Panamanian. The man's

girlfriend showed up in Colombia, desperately trying to find him in hospitals and morgues. Eventually, she called Miguel for help. He said that her boyfriend must have had an accident, and he would do everything he could to get to the bottom of things. The woman thanked him and said that she was returning to Panama. Miguel insisted that she stay a little longer, so that he could send one of his best men to assist her and escort her home. He said that the name of the man on his way to help her was Memo.

Disturbed by the escalating violence, Jorge resented the god-fathers for ignoring his advice about the mounting threats to the cartel. His predictions had come true and it was only a matter of time before disaster struck completely. With a wife and two children to think about, Jorge desperately wanted to quit his job, but how could he without getting killed?

CHAPTER 11
SAVING PALLOMARI

In prison, the Chess Player contemplated the events that had led to his arrest. One in particular bothered him: the raid on the cartel accountant Pallomari, who had allowed so many damaging documents to fall into the hands of General Serrano. On top of the raid, why had Pallomari given away even more information during police questioning? So far, Miguel had protected Pallomari, but that was now unacceptable. Gilberto received a visit from William, Miguel's son who was being groomed to run the cartel in the absence of the two main godfathers. Gilberto told William that it was time for Pallomari to go.

Miguel delegated the work to a trusted assassin called Yusti, a man of small stature with thinning hair combed to one side. In his thirties, Yusti looked more like a timid bank teller than an assassin. He was an effective killer because people barely noticed him and even if they did, he appeared harmless.

Miguel asked Jorge to help Yusti with the logistics. Hiding his displeasure at getting embroiled in a conspiracy to murder an accountant, Jorge agreed to do everything possible. Refusing to follow the godfathers' orders was a death sentence. If he tried to quit, they would kill him for knowing too much. Jorge had finally realised that his only way out was to bring the entire cartel down. If he did it in pieces, he would be found out and killed. He would go through the motions of working for the cartel with security issues while plotting its destruction.

Yusti met Jorge to discuss Pallomari's murder. Although Pallomari had gone into hiding, he was exposed through his wife, Patricia, who owned a computer business. As she worked in Cali, Yusti assumed correctly that her husband would be living close by. Aware of all of the residences that Pallomari frequented, Jorge remained quiet to stall Yusti.

Jorge was invited to a meeting hosted by another of the godfathers' security coordinators. He declined to go, and warned that the meeting in daylight by a soccer field was foolish. The meeting went ahead in a grandstand. Claiming to have been tipped off by a concerned citizen, troops arrived. The cartel men started ripping intelligence documents and eating the pieces of paper. The troops drew their guns and ordered them to leave the paper intact. Important documents were seized, containing telephone numbers that the Search Bloc had tapped and the licence plates of cars the authorities were tailing. More troops arrived. The men were arrested for espionage and handcuffed.

The news of the arrests angered Miguel because he and Gilberto owned the soccer club. He cursed the security men for getting caught so easily. Asked for his opinion, Jorge said that he had warned the leader of the meeting. Miguel swore at Jorge for having foreknowledge and not preventing the meeting.

Gilberto's arrest followed by the security men getting busted at the grandstand induced paranoia in the cartel. Suspicion fell on Jorge because he had declined to go to the ill-fated meeting. He received a message from the hit man, Yusti, requesting a meeting at an ice-cream vendor by a traffic circle. Jorge wondered whether Miguel had sanctioned a hit on him or if Yusti just wanted to discuss the assassination of Pallomari.

Armed with a pistol, Jorge arrived at the location and watched Yusti park his car. Surrounded by families, they bought ice cream. Yusti wanted an AR-15 rifle. Jorge said that his friend had one. Yusti wanted it immediately, so Jorge claimed that his friend was out of town. For the time being, Yusti agreed to get by with a pistol with a laser sighting.

Although some members of the cartel were suspicious of Jorge, the godfathers dismissed their accusations. Due to the loss of the security men who had been busted at the grandstand, Jorge's duties were increased.

The intelligence reports Jorge received – leaked from the Search Bloc – indicated that the house Pallomari was hiding at was about to be raided. If Pallomari were arrested, he would be killed in custody by police loyal to the cartel. As part of his strategy to exit the cartel, Jorge needed to keep Pallomari alive.

At 3 pm, Jorge showed up at Pallomari's house. The person who answered the door denied any knowledge of Pallomari. Citing the imminent danger to Pallomari's life, Jorge demanded to see the accountant. Arriving at the door and gazing wearily from behind spectacles, the accountant asked why Jorge was there. Citing the Search Bloc's raid, Jorge offered to move him to a safe house. Not trusting Jorge, Pallomari was dismissive. Nervously emerging from a room, Pallomari's two sons watched Jorge, who pointed out that the boys would be safer if their father were absent. Finally relenting, Pallomari packed his luggage, said goodbye to his sons and got in Jorge's car. He was transported to a safe house that Jorge used for listening to calls that the cartel had wiretapped.

The next day after the Search Bloc's raids, Jorge went to collect Pallomari, but he was gone. Jorge was pleased. It was wise of Pallomari to have disappeared. The more precautions he took to stay alive, the more likely that Jorge's exit plan would work.

Mid-1995 saw a record amount of raids on the cartel. The authorities were using information obtained during the raid of Pallomari's office and information from cartel workers incarcerated in Florida. Cartel employees started to surrender just like members of Pablo's organisation had during his wars with the government.

Miguel continued to run the operation. Due to all of the raids, he made extra copies of the names of everyone on the cartel's payroll, including the money they had received and the favours they had pledged. In case he needed them in an emergency, he spread the records throughout various properties.

In June 1995, a wiretap was intercepted concerning preparations for a raid at Miguel's house where he had lived for two years.

Jorge notified Miguel. A captain at the Search Bloc confirmed that the raid was scheduled for 3 pm, just four hours away. With time to spare before the raid, Miguel had a shower and ate before leaving. He left behind a wooden desk with a red hue and a hiding place in its thick top section. Inside were numerous cartel records on paper and disk. A carpenter had manufactured the raid-proof desk, which was about to be tested.

When the Search Bloc troops arrived, a young pool boy said that the owners of the home were on a long vacation in Europe. Could he describe them? No, because he had never met them. The troops searched the house, but did not examine the desk.

With his main residence compromised, Miguel moved into a friend's house, where in-between running the business, he relaxed in a large Jacuzzi. He also moved over the desk. Confident of its ability to withstand raids, he filled it with even more sensitive information. Jorge worried about the authorities discovering the contents of the desk. If prosecutors got their hands on the information, the entire cartel would be in jeopardy. After contemplating warning Miguel, he thought better of it. If the entire cartel fell, then he would finally be free of his job.

With nothing linking him to his new hideout, Miguel felt so safe that he started to invite over guests, including one of his wives and an ex-priest he had pinned negotiation hopes on. Perhaps the ex-priest's allies would support him in secret talks with officials. As the ex-priest travelled down a cul-de-sac in Garden City to Miguel's new home, he was followed by undercover DEA agents.

Early the next day, a helicopter was dispatched as part of a raid. Taken by surprise, Miguel had no time to evacuate the premises. He got inside a specially designed compartment below the Jacuzzi, which contained the heating system and plumbing. With claustrophobia setting in, he experienced hot flashes and nausea.

Stationed near Miguel's home, Jorge heard a helicopter and realised that a raid was in progress. He drove towards Miguel's. From a safe distance, he watched the police surround the residence. He ordered all of Miguel's bodyguards to evacuate the area as they were a tell-tale sign of the godfather's presence.

Inside an SUV with dark windows, the two DEA agents, Chris and Dave, monitored the raid and listened to the action on a radio. The Palestinian-American DEA agent had been allowed to participate in the raid because his skin colour made him appear Colombian.

In the house, the police discovered four people: Miguel's fourth wife, a cartel aide, a driver and a maid. The presence of the first two gave hope of finding Miguel. But after two hours, the police grew bored. Assuming that Miguel had been warned in advance and had fled, the police departed. The media photographed them leaving, including the DEA agent Salameh.

After getting summoned to Miguel's hideout, Jorge parked in the garage and closed the door. He opened the rear of the car and politely asked Miguel to get in. Feeling ill and grumpy, Miguel reluctantly climbed inside.

Relocating Miguel allowed Jorge to stall the plot to kill Pallomari. He assumed that Pallomari was safe until a security aide told Jorge that Pallomari and his wife were about to be eliminated. They wanted the wife gone because she knew too much about the cartel. Miguel's son William had told the aide about the plot.

Jorge suspected that the hit had been reassigned because he had stalled it. Excluded, he could no longer save Pallomari. To reinsert himself, he tried to arrange a meeting with Yusti, but was told that the hit man was busy on other assassinations. He contemplated how to alert the US government without incurring a death sentence.

Miguel established himself in the house of the attractive widow of one of the cartel's victims. She didn't know that Miguel had sanctioned the hit on her husband, who had worked for the cartel. With romance blossoming, Miguel acted like a father to the widow's five-year-old daughter. He paid for the widow to have liposuction and sent flowers to the clinic. After the godfather promised to buy her a new property, Jorge drove them to look at ranches and vacation homes. The five-year-old shrieking in a room drew Jorge's attention. He found Miguel on all fours, pretending to be a horse giving her a ride. The grimace Miguel flashed told Jorge to keep the play a secret. Diversions from cartel business usually irritated Miguel, but in the company of the widow, he was uncharacteristically happy.

With Miguel at the widow's house, a more permanent hideout was installed with communications technology and a hidden compartment in its walls. Accessible from the living room, the hiding space was behind a small bathroom. Phone technology at the hideout enabled conference calls and clients on hold to listen to music. A phone company executive who wore a gold Rolex, expensive white shoes and imported aftershave engineered the telephone lines to go through a switching device that prevented eavesdropping and tracing. As a decoy, the device made Miguel's calls seem to originate from a distant building.

In mid-1995, two disasters struck the cartel. The godfathers' primary source of information at the Search Bloc failed a polygraph test. The disgraced sergeant joined the cartel's security apparatus, but he was unable to establish a new source of information within the Search Bloc because his former colleagues shunned him.

With the authorities searching for him in Cali, godfather Chepe relocated to Bogotá. The government was offering $625,000 for his capture, so that he could face drugs and terrorism charges. He made overtures to General Serrano to turn himself in. On July 4, 1995, the burly godfather with distinctive thick brows and greying hair and a moustache went to eat at the Carbon de Pollo restaurant, near the general's home, but the general never showed up.

While dining, Chepe was approached and arrested. The official story was that he had been recognised by a bodyguard of General Serrano and arrested by two policemen. Capitalising on Chepe's propensity for fine food, the general claimed to have posted his men in several fancy restaurants, and as luck would have it, the plan had worked. The general never explained why he had put his men in restaurants by his own house as opposed to restaurants in Cali, which the godfather frequented. It seems that Chepe was surrendering to Serrano, but the general had double-crossed him to get the $625,000 reward. If Chepe had surrendered, the money would not have been forthcoming. When it comes to large sums of money provided by US taxpayers, foreign governments come up with all kinds of strategies to obtain it by pretending to fight the War on Drugs.

A fingerprint check confirmed Chepe's identity. In a denim jacket and white trousers, he was paraded in front of the media at police headquarters. The National Police put him in a brown armchair, where he sat in silence as cameras flashed, his expression grim and determined, his brown eyes roaming the room. Eventually, he was hustled away by men in suits and police in green uniforms. Following his arrest, more cartel workers turned themselves in to capitalise on the leniency offered to surrendering criminals.

The DEA announced that Chepe was one of the most violent members of the Cali Mafia, and an expert manager of worldwide cocaine distribution, as well as production and money laundering. The agency hailed his arrest as a victory in the War on Drugs: "The arrest of [Chepe] in Bogota, Colombia last night is another crippling blow to the Cali Mafia. Coupled with the arrest last month of Gilberto Rodriguez Orejuela, this action by the Colombian National Police demonstrates that the Cali Mafia is not invincible. [Chepe] has long been a vicious player in the international cocaine trade, and his arrest is welcome news to the DEA."

The DEA hoped that "the Colombian Government would keep up the momentum" and continue their efforts against the Cali Mafia. "In its war against the Cali drug Mafia, the Colombian Government is to be commended for this arrest, and for the recent arrest of Gilberto Rodriguez Orejuela. However, major Mafia leaders like [Chepe] and [Gilberto] must be prosecuted and punished to the extent commensurate with their nefarious criminal activities, and cannot be permitted to manage their operations from prison."

Some US lawyers had been conveying threats from the godfathers to cartel workers arrested in America. Several of the lawyers were indicted on conspiracy and racketeering charges. One was Joel Rosenthal, a lawyer Jorge previously had dealings with. After Jorge read about Rosenthal's arrest, he realised that another piece of his plan to escape from the cartel had materialised. He assumed that Rosenthal, facing a large sentence, would have no choice but to cooperate, and Jorge held the key that the DEA was seeking.

To call Rosenthal securely, Jorge drove to a mall and entered a phone booth. As the phone rang, Jorge knew that if the call was successful there would be no turning back. The call went to a messaging system that said Rosenthal's offices were closed. Jorge left his pager number and a message that he was on Rosenthal's side.

Within an hour, Jorge's pager beeped with a Miami number. Back in the booth and on the phone, Jorge said that he would be glad to help Rosenthal get his sentence reduced. Rosenthal handed the phone to a DEA agent. The agent was aware of Jorge because Rosenthal had identified him as a possible cartel defector. Jorge was third on the agent's Cali watch-list. The agent told Jorge that he was about to be indicted and he was in big trouble for his cartel activity, but he could save himself by handing over Miguel.

Jorge said that could be done at any time because he always knew Miguel's whereabouts, but firstly, he wanted the DEA to save Pallomari before the cartel killed him. Unaware of Pallomari, the agent asked for an explanation. Jorge explained the significance of Pallomari. Satisfied with Jorge's responses, the agent wanted Jorge to meet his DEA colleagues in Colombia: Chris and Dave. Even though he knew that the US Embassy in Colombia had been compromised by the cartel, Jorge agreed.

Using a phone at a hairdresser's salon, Jorge organised a meeting with Chris and Dave near the main gate of the International

Centre for Tropical Agriculture, where a Colombian talking to Americans would not be considered unusual. Concerned that Jorge was setting them up to be assassinated, the agents arrived early to scope out the location. Stationed in a car by a sugarcane field, they watched Jorge arrive and park. He emerged from his car alone and displayed his hands to show he was unarmed. As he approached, they joked about him looking like Sean Connery.

Jorge opened the passenger door and got in the front of their car. Noticing their blonde hair and blue eyes, he felt relief as his life could not be trusted with Colombians. With the agents constantly checking the surroundings and their mirrors, Jorge sensed how nervous they were. On the backseat, Dave asked if it were true that Jorge could help them capture Miguel. Of course he could. They asked how that was possible. As the head of Miguel's security, Jorge could deliver the godfather to the DEA at any time, but first, they needed to save Pallomari. Despite their lack of knowledge about Pallomari, Jorge instinctively trusted the agents.

For over two hours, Jorge described Miguel's routines, habits and security arrangements. They would know they had located him by clues at the property, including Panasonic telephone equipment, the fruit and vegetable juices he ate for hypoglycaemia and his Mazda 626. Putting his life in the agents' hands, he warned them not to trust anyone in the Search Bloc, which the cartel had compromised.

Asked why he was cooperating, Jorge said that he had been hired to prevent attacks by Pablo Escobar, but since then he had seen the cartel in a different light due to all of the violence and corruption. Upon trying to get out of the cartel, he had realised he was trapped and the lives of his entire family were at risk.

The agents asked Jorge many questions to try to trip him up to determine whether he was authentic. In the end, they were as impressed with him as he was with them. Their priority though was Miguel. They wanted to capture Miguel now and save Pallomari later.

CHAPTER 12
TRAPPING MIGUEL

Jorge gave Miguel's address to the DEA agents. As it was an eight-storey building, he would get back to them with the exact apartment number as he didn't know whether Miguel was on the second or the fourth floor. He drew a map of the area, highlighting the bodyguards stationed near a river. Before parting, they exchanged telephone codes to be used on pagers. They codenamed their new informant Connery.

With many of his lieutenants having surrendered and the government offering a substantial reward for information leading to his capture, Miguel was unable to run the cartel as usual. There were no more visits from politicians, priests and senior police officials. Miguel couldn't let anyone know where he lived including his own bodyguards, who were stationed away from the building.

Jorge knew that Miguel worked late into the night. To determine which apartment Miguel was in, Jorge staked out the building. In the small hours, all of the lights in the apartments went out except for one on the fourth floor, which stayed on until 4 am. To doublecheck, Jorge made a call while watching the apartment. The lights came on as a phone was answered. Jorge told one of Miguel's aides that all of the bodyguards were in place and he was going home.

On a Thursday, Jorge arranged to meet the agents at a construction site at a new mall. Amid bricks, mud and industrial equipment, the agents revealed that they had located two apartments in the building registered in the names of cartel associates: 402 and 801. Jorge narrowed it down to 402. The agents wanted to raid the apartment by Saturday morning in case Miguel decided to relocate. Jorge drew a map to demonstrate the best approach for the troops to enter the building. Things were moving so fast, Jorge braced to tell his wife and other family members that they were going to have to evacuate the country for their safety.

At the next meeting with the agents, Jorge showed up in black clothes. Trying to conceal his nerves, he suggested they drive by Miguel's apartment. As they got closer to Miguel's, the agents realised how problematic approaching the building would be for the troops because nobody went down the street unless they had a destination there. Dozens of troops raiding the building by surprise only seemed possible if they arrived at 5 am when the godfather was asleep.

The raid was planned in secrecy. The local Search Bloc was excluded. The warrant submitted to the attorney general's office stated that the raid was on a lab that was manufacturing precursor chemicals for cocaine. The troops travelled overnight from Bogotá, unaware of the nature of their work.

Prior to the raid, Jorge told Miguel's bodyguards in the area to be alert. If security was lax, the godfather might hold Jorge accountable. On his way home, he prayed for himself, his family and Pallomari. Just as Jorge was dozing, his pager beeped. It was Miguel. Jorge left his house to call on a private phone. A contact in Bogotá had informed Miguel about a raid that was due in the morning. Jorge asked if he knew where or when. Miguel was sure they hadn't located him. He told Jorge and his men to stay vigilant.

The information leak terrified Jorge. If the raid had been compromised, what else did the leaker know? With his mind in turmoil, Jorge wondered whether it would be best to stop the raid. First of all, he needed to follow Miguel's orders. He beefed up security, and sent spies to the Search Bloc's gates. He ordered an aide to prevent any hostile traffic from travelling down Miguel's road. He left a voicemail on the agents' pager, warning them to stop the dinner because it wouldn't be a surprise party. He returned home, got in bed and realised that if the raid were halted then suspicion would fall upon him. He didn't know which was worse:

allowing the raid to proceed or calling it off. Instead of taking any further action, he prayed and waited for his radiophone to ring.

In the darkness of a parking lot at a pizza restaurant, the raid party arrived from Bogotá. Having missed Jorge's voicemail, the agents were proceeding. In the presence of a federal prosecutor with a search warrant, the agents told the heavily armed policemen that the target was a chemical-manufacturing lab. To approach the house undetected, the police were told to get into two chicken-transportation trucks. Their complaints about the stink were drowned out as the trucks rumbled away with a DEA agent in each. To prevent the cartel lookouts from growing suspicious, the trucks snaked around Cali. As they drew near to Miguel's, they slowed down.

Shortly after 4 am, a burly bodyguard on a motorbike spotted the two trucks and grabbed his radiophone. He yelled for Miguel's aide to wake up and he sped after the trucks. Watching the police surround the building, he called Jorge, who instructed all of the bodyguards to put away their radios, leave the area and rendez-vous at a petrol station. Alerted by his aide, Miguel disappeared into a hiding place.

At the petrol station, Jorge took charge. He commended the bodyguard for spotting the trucks. He ordered radio silence, and, in the event of an emergency, the use of a new radio channel. To prevent the authorities from breaching the cartel's communica-tions, he had an engineer remotely turn off Miguel's radiophones. Jorge went home.

The absence of a chemical lab inside the apartment required some explaining to the troops. Upon being told by the agents that the raid was to locate the boss of the Cali Cartel, the troops refused to participate unless Colombian law was being observed. They wanted the Search Bloc contacted to provide backup.

Twenty minutes later, about fifty troops arrived from the Search Bloc, including a captain on the cartel's payroll. The prose-cutor from Bogotá claimed that the search warrant was incorrect, and that a local prosecutor was needed with a valid warrant, who would monitor the raid. It took almost an hour for the Cali prosecutor's office to dispatch a prosecutor friendly to Miguel.

Almost two hours after they had arrived, Chris and Dave watched in despair as the raid commenced. Inside, the troops found the tell-tale signs of Miguel that Jorge had described: his preferred food and drinks, a Panasonic phone system, a Mazda 626 in the garage... They also found two housekeepers and Miguel's aide. The agents congratulated each other on finding the right place, but after two hours of searching the troops were giving up. Assuming that Miguel was in a secret compartment, the agents had checked all of the walls, but had detected nothing.

Expecting to hear news of Miguel's arrest, Jorge waited by his phone. Each passing hour raised his blood pressure. By 8 am, Jorge assumed that Miguel had slipped away, and that the cartel's focus would now be on identifying and eliminating the informant. Unable to sit still, he headed to the raid.

By 9 am, Jorge had parked by a river opposite Miguel's neighbourhood. Some of the bodyguards he had ordered to leave were gathered near the raid. One of them was an aide who had suspected Jorge of setting up the men who had been arrested at the grandstand. Concerned that the authorities would capture them, Jorge withheld his frustration rather than risk getting in an argument with the aide.

Asked for an update by Jorge, the aide said that Miguel was in the building and the troops had found the correct apartment. How could he be sure? Miguel's son William had told him. Concerned about William launching a witch-hunt for the informant, Jorge wanted to get closer to him, so he asked the aide for William's whereabouts. William was running operations out of Benito's Bakery in central Cali. Jorge felt that the aide was going to cause trouble for him.

Near the bakery, Jorge was crossing the road when a car parked nearby. Miguel's sister asked Jorge to come to the car. Exasperated, she asked what he knew.

"The raid caught us all by surprise," Jorge said. "One of my men alerted Miguel before the troops arrived. He could have gotten away. He could have hidden."

She was praying that they would catch him and respect his life. That would end the family's nightmare. Her biggest fear was her brothers ending up like Pablo Escobar. Jorge said he understood. Hopefully, if Miguel escaped from the raid then a surrender would be worked out. Jorge and his men would do everything to protect Miguel.

After the sister departed, Jorge found William sitting outside the bakery at a table, his bodyguards maintaining a safe distance. He asked William how it had happened. Shaking his head, William said he was hopeful and that Jorge shouldn't jump to conclusions. Miguel had probably hidden. After feigning surprise at the news of a hiding place, Jorge briefed William on Miguel's late-night call about the imminent raid. On Miguel's orders, he had beefed up security. Having spotted the chicken trucks, one of his lookouts had alerted Miguel just in time.

Jorge was getting into his stride convincing William about the sincerity of his efforts when a pager vibrated in his pocket that indicated a DEA message. He told William that he had to use the toilet. In a cubicle, he extracted the pager, which showed a phone number. He decided to risk using the bakery telephone because it was in a private area and he could see if anyone was coming. The agents were at a Pizza Hut, awaiting his call. As soon as the phone rang, Chris grabbed it.

Jorge revealed that Miguel was hiding in a compartment. He was absolutely sure. They should focus on a small bathroom by the living room. With five bathrooms to choose from, the agents said that they would focus on the powder room, where they had discovered that the cabinet doors had been installed so close to the toilet that they had banged it when opened.

Jorge returned to William, who was surrounded by his inner circle, whom Jorge referred to as the Brothers Four. William's greeting raised Jorge's guard. He told Jorge the good news that Miguel had escaped. Jorge congratulated William and sat down.

Surely William feeding him fake information meant that they suspected him of informing. They were trying to trick him into passing the information onto the agents.

A messenger showed up with the keys to a hideout and stated that it was ready for Miguel. William instructed the messenger to give the keys to Jorge, who dismissed the idea by stating that he didn't know the area. The messenger said that the building was so tall that it could not be missed. With his life in the balance, Jorge needed to put on a good show. He ordered the messenger to shut up because they were in a public place and not to be so careless. He told him to give the keys to a man at the next table. After organising a car for the garage at Miguel's new hideout, he ordered one of William's friends to ensure the apartment was ready, and not to share the address with anyone.

Jorge was back in his swing, and even wondering whether he had been paranoid about William earlier. Then the DEA pager vibrated again. This time he ignored it. He waited until his usual lunchtime, and said that he was going home for an hour to eat with his family. Jorge drove to a hotel with phones in its lobby. He paged the agents. A phone rang. They still hadn't located Miguel. Having never been in the apartment, Jorge couldn't describe the hiding space. He wanted the agents to enter the apartments above and below 402 to help identify any anomalies in Miguel's powder room.

At home, Jorge was greeted by the delicious smells of garlic and onions, but he was too nervous to eat. The salsa music on the radio was halted for an announcement: Miguel had been arrested. As his neighbours were cartel members, Jorge hid his relief. His appetite returned, so he poured some soup.

The music halted again for a second announcement: the earlier announcement was incorrect: Miguel had not been arrested.

Jorge shoved the soup away and returned to the bakery. William had left, so Jorge performed his usual security rounds. He contacted an engineer to check that Miguel's radiophones had been remotely disabled. To prevent rumours of him liaising with

DEA agents, he wanted to be seen by as many cartel members as possible.

Jorge's DEA pager vibrated. On the phone, the agents conceded that even though they had the utmost confidence in Jorge and that they knew Miguel was there, the search was probably going to be abandoned as they had achieved nothing in seven hours. The police captain and the troops had run out of patience. Most of the police were watching a football game on a large TV in one of the bedrooms. According to the prosecutors, the legal limits of the search had been reached.

Jorge hadn't wanted to disclose the nature of Miguel's special desk until the godfather had been apprehended, but now he felt he had no choice, so he revealed that if they broke open the reddish desk they would find Miguel's treasure. Surely that would boost the morale of the raiding party. He urged them not to give up on accessing Miguel in the powder-room wall.

Continuing his security work to calm his nerves, Jorge hoped that the next DEA message would be news of Miguel's arrest. He practised feigning concern for the loss of the boss, and taking a lead role in the hunt for the informant. Hours later, his pager vibrated…

After finding the desk, the agents opened its drawers, felt its surfaces and crawled underneath it, all of which perplexed them. Out of the four agents, Salameh managed to lift the desk and tip it over. It cracked open with an explosive noise that drew the football spectators into the room. A broken drawer revealed three leather briefcases with Miguel's treasure.

A captain on the cartel's payroll asked what the agents were doing and who had told them about the desk. They ignored him, while gathering the briefcases, and placing the documents on a dining table. They found a cancelled cheque for President Ernesto's campaign, a list of contact details for cartel workers, evidence of various payments made to the police, politicians and the media… The Colombian commander in charge of the operation said that he needed to get everything to the head of the National Police.

With an aide, he collected the documents and left the building.

The discovery of the stash enthused the agents enough to start drilling through the walls around the powder room, while the police resumed watching football on the TV. With the commander gone, the captain attempted to thwart the agents' efforts. Spotting urine on the floor, the agents assumed that it was part of the sabotage, so rather than avoid the urine, they investigated it. On his hands and knees, Chris put his head into a floor cabinet and yelled that he had discovered something unusual. They found an oxygen tube going into the wall behind the sink. Drilling revealed airspace between the walls. Unable to find an access door, they needed a sledgehammer.

Just as Miguel was about to be found, a little man with black hair and a typewriter entered the apartment. As the head of the regional attorney general's office, he had more legal power than the other two prosecutors present. He yelled at everybody to cease the search. Approaching the Americans, he demanded to know who they were, what they were doing and under whose authority. He locked the front door and pocketed the key. Upset by the intruder, Chris said they were operating with the Colombian National Police, acting on information that Miguel was in the building. After putting his typewriter on the dining table, the prosecutor said the agents had no right to raid Colombians and damage private property. Typing at a rapid speed, he produced an official document that charged the agents with an unlawful search.

Losing his cool, Dave yelled that Miguel was right behind the wall. The prosecutor requested the agents' ID papers. After being told that they were not under arrest, they tried to leave, but the door was locked. The prosecutor refused to let them out. They demanded a call to the US embassy. The prosecutor threatened to arrest them for carrying guns. The embassy was contacted. The prosecutor handed them a complaint, which they refused to sign. After much wrangling over legal issues, they were allowed to leave with their weapons.

Chris and Dave dreaded breaking the news of the failed raid to Jorge. They feared for his life. Surely the cartel was on the verge of eliminating him as a suspected informant. Hearing the news from the agents, Jorge figured that he was dead. They explained that they had been forced to leave even though they were so close. They apologised for letting him down. Jorge requested that the building be guarded around-the-clock so that Miguel could not escape. The agents had requested overnight security. They offered to move Jorge and his family from the country for their protection. As his work wasn't over, Jorge declined.

On the drive home, Jorge imagined that William suspected him. He wanted to hide like Pallomari, but instead, he decided to play a lead role in investigating who had leaked Miguel's whereabouts.

After he had parked, a voice cried out from the darkness across the road, demanding to speak to him. The chubby man leaning on a motorbike was the aide whom Jorge trusted the most. He asked if Jorge knew about the meeting. Unknown to Jorge, William had convened an emergency security meeting without inviting him. It was scheduled to start at around 10 pm at Angel's disco. Angel was a trafficker with his own team of hit men. He had built the reddish desk that the agents had cracked open. As a close friend of Miguel, he was likely to transfer William's mistrust of Jorge to Miguel. If Jorge didn't attend the meeting, his actions would be criticised without him having the opportunity for rebuttal. While his aide waited, he changed and washed his face.

Jorge was still at home when his pager beeped. Miguel's aide wanted him to call apartment 402. He dialled and Miguel answered. Jorge praised God for keeping Miguel safe. The godfather wanted Jorge to rescue him from apartment 402, which was completely surrounded by the police. Miguel's rescue plan involved Jorge showing up and identifying himself as a concerned citizen who had arranged the delivery of up to sixty meals for the police. While the troops were tucking in, Miguel could slip away. Instinctively, Jorge disliked the plan. Perhaps it was the product of Miguel being entombed in a hiding space for too long. With Miguel pushed to breaking point, Jorge simply agreed rather than risk incurring the godfather's wrath.

Due to the call from Miguel, Jorge and his aide arrived late at the security meeting. Upstairs in the nightclub, William was on a chair in the middle of the dancefloor surrounded by ten associates. Their icy reception made Jorge wonder whether they had been discussing him.

Jorge sat in a chair and took control of the meeting by announcing Miguel's call. He detailed the plan to order meals for the police, and warned that it probably wouldn't work. It could end up with arrests and unwanted media exposure. William agreed to tell his father to change the plan. Leaning back, Jorge noticed his hands were trembling and that he had sweated through his shirt. Had the others noticed?

The new plan involved rescue teams around the building. If Miguel could traverse the steep hill at the back of the apartment, they could pick him up at the highway. The obstacles included the sheer length of the slope, the prickly vegetation and Miguel's age and poor health.

They were ruminating on the plan when William received a call from a Search Bloc captain on the cartel's payroll. Having received a call from Miguel, the captain said getting the godfather out of the apartment was impossible due to the police. Unable to contain his anger, William reminded the captain that taking cartel money had never been impossible. This was the moment for repayment. He needed to find a way. William swore and hung up. Asked whether the captain would help, William said to count him out. They would rescue Miguel themselves. William picked up the phone. Miguel accepted the challenge of getting up the slope.

After midnight, the rescue team travelled to the road behind the apartment. Jorge and his aide pulled over, parked and raised the hood of the car as if they had broken down. Every now and then, another rescuer joined them and pretended to help with the car problem. As soon as Miguel headed for the slope, they would send a rescuer down to assist him.

Before the plan was fully in effect, the corrupt captain called. He had moved Miguel to a new hideout by hiding the godfather in the back of his car. Dozens of armed police had watched him leave. A party at dawn celebrated the captain's achievement. The news reported Miguel's escape. An inspection of the apartment revealed the hiding space with its door open, an oxygen tank and a blood-stained shirt, indicating that the drill had penetrated the godfather. The news reported the clash between the prosecutor and the American agents who had overstepped their authority.

As the cartel interrogated suspected informants, Jorge was assigned to interview Miguel's aide, who had been present during the raid. Miguel instructed Jorge to take with him Valencia, a former sergeant and intelligence expert. Jorge picked up Valencia and Dario, a friend of William, in a car with a recording device running. By stopping on the journey and getting out of the car, Jorge hope to record Valencia and Dario speaking freely about him, perhaps expressing any of the cartel's concerns.

An hour later, they started questioning the aide, who was suffering from hunger and sleep deprivation. The aide expressed concern for Miguel. Despite the DEA agents' attempts to trick him into talking, the aide had revealed nothing. He had overheard the agents stating that the informant was knowledgeable about the apartment. The informant was a woman the agents had referred to as Patricia. She had provided details about Miguel's desk.

Jorge asked which women had visited the apartment. None on the aide's shift. Knowing that his name would not be raised, Jorge asked for the names of everyone else who had visited the apartment. The aide was advised to avoid the authorities because he was eligible to be arrested for harbouring a fugitive now that it was obvious that Miguel had been in the hiding place.

After Jorge dropped off his colleagues, he listened to the recording. Having noticed his nervousness, they had expressed their distrust of him. While Jorge was absent, they had heard his DEA pager vibrating and decided that they were being recorded. As Valencia coveted Jorge's job, Jorge was fearful of him inciting distrust to pave the way for Jorge's elimination, which would create a job opportunity. Once again, Chris and Dave offered to extricate Jorge from the cartel, but he refused.

Jorge was at home with his wife when his phone rang. In a hostile tone, Miguel announced that he was concerned about him because he had behaved nervously on the day of the raid. Assuming that William, Valencia and Dario were conspiring to oust him, Jorge admitted that he had been nervous because he was in charge of Miguel's safety and he felt that he had let the godfather down. How could he not have been nervous with such a great responsibility? Jorge apologised for failing the godfather. He listed the additional security measures he had taken, and reminded Miguel that one of his men had raised the alarm in time for the godfather to hide. After mulling over the response in silence, Miguel agreed with Jorge.

Due to the close call with the agents, Miguel's security was rearranged. Jorge would only be responsible for perimeter security, including monitoring the police and setting up surveillance posts by river bridges. Miguel's new hideout was in a tiny area by the Cali River and the mountains. Miguel instructed Jorge not to enter the area or even to patrol streets north of the river.

Unknown to Jorge, Miguel was in a building called Hacienda Buenos Aires, a high-rise with nineteen floors, which contained luxury apartments up to 4,000 square feet. Miguel's apartment had marble floors. He had added an exercise bike, a pool table and lots of phone lines.

Jorge was in a race to pinpoint Miguel's location before the cartel identified him as the informant. If the former occurred first, Jorge and his family would immediately be relocated to the USA. The consequences of losing the race were unthinkable. Unable to enter Miguel's neighbourhood, Jorge had a friend drive there and collect the addresses of the two locations at the top of a list of likely premises which Jorge had prepared.

Paranoid about being under surveillance by the cartel, Jorge took extra precautions one evening to scout out the likely buildings. He ended up on a hill to the rear of the neighbourhood. Taking photos, he noticed a seven-foot-deep flood control channel, which would provide ideal access for the authorities to sneak up on Miguel's hideout.

On his next call to the agents, Jorge disclosed that Miguel was in a new property, which only four people knew about. He'd narrowed it down to two buildings, but didn't know which floor or apartment. He'd mailed them photos of the buildings. They expressed concern about his safety. Jorge responded that although he was a suspect, Miguel did not believe that he was the informant. In the following days, Jorge and the agents assigned the highest probability to Miguel residing in Hacienda Buenos Aires because the building had been registered in the name of a cartel associate.

Not wanting anything to go wrong on the next raid, Jorge met Chris and Dave near a sugarcane field by a quiet road to discuss strategy. Some taxis passing by slowed-down, which disturbed the agents. The group moved further away from the road. Jorge was showing them maps and photos of the building when the police arrived in a van. Both agents tossed their guns into the sugarcane. One hid the photos under his front seat. Knowing he would end up dead if he were arrested with the agents, Jorge approached the five policemen emerging from the van with machine guns. Smiling, he asked if he could help them.

After studying Jorge and the Americans to see if they were armed, the lieutenant stated that they were investigating the murder of a taxi driver. What was Jorge doing there? Having not seen anything suspicious in the area, Jorge was merely talking to his friends: two Americans who worked at the International Center for Tropical Agriculture. They didn't want any trouble.

The lieutenant insisted on searching the cars. Dreading them finding the photos of Miguel's new residence under the driver's seat of the agents' car, Jorge enticed the policemen towards his own vehicle by opening the back and urging them to look inside to see that they were not traffickers or murderers. As they examined the car, Jorge remembered that he had stashed illegal cartel radios in a wheel well.

The policemen were more enthused about questioning the Americans. The agents claimed to be employees of the International Center for Tropical Agriculture, meeting their friend after work. The police wanted their work IDs. Jorge offered his ID, while the Americans pretended to search for theirs. One of the agents managed to give Jorge $650 in bribery money. Taking the lieutenant to one side, Jorge said that the Americans were embarrassed. Offering the money, he said to take it and forget about them. Refusing the money, the lieutenant insisted on searching the Americans' car. Chris objected that they had not broken any laws. The lieutenant asked why they were trying to bribe him if they had done nothing wrong. Growing angry, Chris asked whether the lieutenant had better things to do such as catching thieves.

Jorge whispered to the lieutenant that the Americans were embarrassed because they were actually homosexuals meeting for a liaison. Rather than subject them to a scandal, wouldn't the lieutenant just be glad to take the money? He held out $650. The lieutenant conferred with his sergeant, who collected the money. The police left. After the agents recovered their guns, Jorge drove away relieved that a disaster had been avoided.

Running security duties, Jorge was stationed at the Intercontinental Hotel. On August 4, 1995, just before 10 pm, he was in the lobby with his second-in-command, Dario. After his DEA pager vibrated, Jorge made the excuse of having to call his wife. He watched Dario leave through the glass doors and join two lookouts on motorbikes posted outside.

On one of the many hotel phones, Jorge called Chris and Dave. They said something had happened, and he had a decision to make. Miguel's hideout had been identified by the agents, who had used binoculars to examine the high-rise. They had spotted two of Miguel's female staff members in white outfits on the 10th floor. To raid the correct floor and not give away the element of surprise, the agents needed to know whether the bottom of the building was the first or the ground floor.

Unable to provide an answer, Jorge pledged to find out. He had been working on removing a cartel contact in the telephone company. He'd told a friend in the military that the telephone worker had performed a number of services for Miguel. The arrest of the telephone worker would increase Miguel's vulnerability.

Not wanting the raid to turn into another legal fiasco, the agents met the attorney general, who granted them a friendly prosecutor and a warrant to smash down Miguel's door. The raid would be conducted by an incorruptible Colombian navy special forces unit. The absence of the Search Bloc would prevent any leaks to Miguel.

Everything had been prepared for the raid ahead of Jorge's schedule. A political scandal had hastened events. Under arrest, President Samper's campaign treasurer had confirmed the god-fathers' contributions to the presidential campaign. Forced to resign, the Defence Minister had been arrested and replaced with a general who was a friend of Miguel's. The general had requested a list of all joint drug operations to be provided within days, which would, no doubt, end up in Miguel's hands.

Chris and Dave wanted to raid Miguel's residence that night. Out of consideration for Jorge's safety, they would postpone the raid if Jorge thought it was prudent. Jorge had not gathered enough intelligence to be able to confirm that Miguel was on the 10th floor. He was anxious about mistakes being made and Miguel slipping away. The consequences would be fatal. The news about the general motivated Jorge to approve of an immediate raid.

After hanging up the phone, Jorge re-joined Dario. By train-ing Dario in security operations, Jorge had created a fall guy out of one of William's friends. The telephone company worker would serve as another fall guy.

While Jorge slept in a state of nervous exhaustion, a sedan led three delivery trucks covered by canvas towards Miguel's residence. Inside were a prosecutor dressed in a blouse and trousers, twelve commandos and twenty policemen, mostly in SWAT-team body armour, some in plainclothes. Before 4 am, the convoy parked on a dark hillside. Traversing a 300-foot slope of rough land, the commandos disturbed a pair of young lovers, who fled after getting searched for weapons and radios. Chris and Dave led the raiding party along a quarter mile of drainage channel with tall concrete walls. The troops were invisible in the darkness, but dogs started barking.

The channel brought them to a hillside not far from the tall white high-rise. Down on his belly, Dave grabbed binoculars and surveyed the 10th floor. The lights were off. Eventually, everyone on the raiding party caught up with the agents. The tough Mexican-American agent Prieto had assisted the exasperated prosecutor in high heels. She chastised them for not warning her about the mountain climbing. After apologising, Chris asked everyone to crowd around him in the channel bed. He said they were there to capture someone on the 10th floor: the leader of the Cali Cartel. The troops were enthusiastic, but the prosecutor was upset at only learning this now. Fearing heights, she was wary of the last leg of the journey: a dangerously steep slope. Chris reversed course to hide in his sedan to keep an eye on Miguel's lookouts on the street. Armed with a radio and binoculars, Dave remained hillside to monitor the raid. Batman and Robin braced to descend into the darkness and lead the troops down the slope.

Within minutes of setting off, the raid party encountered a near vertical drop. Prieto warned that someone's neck would get broken. Armed with a sledgehammer, Salameh said that they had no choice but to proceed. After instructing Prieto to wait with the prosecutor, Salameh jumped. For a short stretch, Salameh managed to slide and skid on his boots. After twenty feet, he fell. Propelled by gravity, he continued on his rear, until his body no longer touched the slope. Creating an avalanche of dirt and gravel, he cascaded.

In his car, Chris was expecting a radio call to confirm that the troops were about to enter the building. Instead, he received an urgent request for help from Salameh, who was at the building. Chris started his engine. Hoping that one person in a car driving slowly would go unnoticed by Miguel's sentries, Chris took his time even though he could feel his blood pumping. Approaching the entrance to the building, he anticipated seeing the entire raid party, but only Salameh was there. Gazing at the dark hillside, Chris could not see the troops stranded on the slope. He asked where everybody was.

Four troops emerged, making six people at the building's entrance. Salameh pointed out that they needed to launch the raid immediately as Miguel could be alerted at any second. To make up the numbers, the two agents would have to participate. One of the four policemen couldn't join in because he had apprehended two night watchmen. The raid would consist of five men.

Under instructions to only observe the raid and to let the Colombians assault the building, Chris felt that he now had no choice but to participate. With all eyes on him, he gave the go-ahead, instructing everyone to take the stairs. Salameh picked up the sledgehammer. They rushed up the stairs to the 10th floor.

Miguel's first line of defence was a thick wooden door. With the Colombians supposedly taking the lead, the sledgehammer was passed to a policeman. The agents stepped aside. The blow banged loud enough to wake up Miguel, but the sledgehammer just bounced off the wood. With no time to waste, Salameh grabbed the sledgehammer and assaulted the door, each time knocking it open a bit wider. From his vantage point, Dave sent a radio message to warn that some of the lights in the apartment had come on. The agents imagined Miguel disappearing into a compartment. The third strike opened the door.

In the dark entrance not knowing where they were going, the

troops dashed over the white marble floor and charged into the enormous apartment in different directions. Feeling his way along a wall, Chris tried to find a light switch. Eventually, he was alone in the kitchen, delighted to see Miguel's Panasonic telephone equipment, which guaranteed that they had raided the correct place. Seeing lights come on in the distance, Chris hastened towards them. He recognised Miguel's driver, whom he and Dave had tailed. He assumed that Miguel had hidden by now until he heard a policeman yell that he'd got him.

"Who found me?" Miguel said. "How did they do it?"

Desperate to see whether Miguel had really been captured, Chris rushed down a hall and through a bedroom and into an enormous closet, where a huge commando was holding a short man, wearing boxers and a T-shirt. Next to them was an eight-inch-thick cement door to a hidden compartment. The commando had grabbed Miguel just in time. The godfather had been halfway into the compartment when the commando had spotted him.

Seeing lanky blonde Chris, Miguel realised that there was DEA involvement. Shedding a perplexed expression, the godfather seemed to accept his fate. Chris scrambled for his radio, and told Dave that they had the godfather. Dave asked if he were sure. Chris said that he was standing right in front of him.

By the time that most of the members of the raiding party had freed themselves from the slope and made it inside, Miguel was seated in the living room in a blue jacket and trousers, wearing handcuffs. The troops took turns to gaze at Miguel. Eventually, the prosecutor arrived in a foul mood, dishevelled and stained by dirt, her high heels broken. Photos were taken of Chris and Dave and Batman and Robin next to Miguel, who remained silent and calm.

Examining the compartment, Chris was amazed by its sophistication. It had an air-conditioning vent, an oxygen tank, water bottles, a folding stool, a bag of peanuts and a copy of Colombia's penal code. The door appeared to be part of the cabinetry. Its steel hinges enabled easy movement. From the inside, it could be locked using four steel rods. Miguel would have been hardly able to move in such an upright coffin. If he had hidden, they never would have found him. The apartment also contained a bonanza of cartel paperwork.

A jeep arrived to transport Miguel. It went too fast for the godfather, who yelled, "Slow down! What's the rush? You already got me."

At 6 am, Jorge's phone rang. His second-in-command, Dario, announced Miguel's capture. Relieved, Jorge feigned surprise. Dario explained that it had happened around 4 am. Jorge asked how it was possible. Dario said that nobody had seen the raiding party approaching the building. They didn't know where they had come from or how they had got in. Jorge wanted to know if there was a rescue plan, but Dario said nothing could be done due to the police and the military. Jorge consoled Dario by stating that he had done his job to the best of his ability.

Later on, Chris thanked Jorge by telephone. The DEA wanted to fly Jorge and his family to America. Jorge refused because of Pallomari. Even though he was now a suspect in Miguel's capture, Jorge wanted to stay undercover until Pallomari was rescued. Due to the increased danger involved, Jorge needed the agents to act fast.

CHAPTER 13
COLOMBIA'S MOST HUNTED

The new acting boss of the Cali Cartel, William, visited his father in prison in Bogotá, where Gilberto and Miguel lived like kings. As well as using cell-phones for business calls, they had rigged a communications network through a prison payphone. With no restrictions on their visitors, family members and lawyers were constantly there. Gilberto received 123 legal visits in one week. Their carpeted cells had cable television, modern stereo equipment and private bathrooms. Their meals were specially prepared. Contraband such as bottles of Scotch and French wine were smuggled in.

Many prisoners employ a skill such as tattooing that they use to earn extra money. In Miguel's case, he opened Poor Miguel's Shop, which sold visitors aspirin, shortbread, drinks and chocolate from Belgium. His entrepreneurship made him eligible for a one third reduction in his sentence.

Back in Cali, William summoned Jorge to a meeting. William's law offices were full of hit men when Jorge arrived. One of Jorge's fall guys, Dario, was there, appearing sorrowful and guilt-ridden for Miguel's capture. William told Jorge that his father's arrest had come about from information provided by the engineer at the telephone company. Jorge was delighted that his other fall guy was getting blamed. William said that Miguel would be fine, and that the godfather's main concern was Pallomari, who must be eliminated immediately. Jorge said that Pallomari had moved. William offered to get an address from Pallomari's lawyer. Jorge said that Yusti had been contracted to do the killing. William objected that he did not know Yusti. He wanted Jorge to find Pallomari right away and to bring him to William.

After tracking Yusti down, Jorge said that William wanted to meet him. In the law offices, Yusti was introduced to William and Pallomari's lawyer. After stating that he'd been ready to kill Pallomari for a long time, Yusti said that the only hold-up had been locating him. William gazed at Pallomari's lawyer for an answer. The lawyer claimed that he didn't remember. Scowling, William told the lawyer that he needed to remember or else he would pay the consequences. Although he didn't know the exact address, the lawyer offered to drive through the neighbourhood to get it. William ordered Jorge, Yusti and Dario to accompany the lawyer, and added that Miguel wanted Pallomari assassinated by the end of the week.

In a small orange Renault, Pallomari's lawyer sped to the South of Cali as if his life depended on it. Pointing at an eight-storey building, he said that Pallomari lived there. Studying the area, Yusti asked which apartment. The lawyer didn't know which apartment or floor, only that Pallomari was in an apartment directly across from the elevator. Jorge offered to research the occupants of every apartment on every floor opposite the elevator. Attempting to stall Yusti, he said it might take a few days. Out to impress William, Yusti was eager to set up surveillance that evening.

With time running out, Chris and Dave came to Cali to meet Jorge at a remote construction site. The agents wanted to know how to approach Pallomari. As the accountant didn't trust Jorge, it was decided that the best bet was through Pallomari's wife, Patricia, an entrepreneur who ran a computer company. Despite the threat to her husband, Patricia had continued to live her life normally. Her company was located near William's law offices. Cartel spies had tailed the striking woman with long dark hair, but her trips to the office and back to home had not led them to Pallomari.

On Tuesday at 6:30 pm, Chris and Dave showed up at the computer company and requested to see Patricia in private. The staff watched as she led them to an office. She sat at a desk and asked what they wanted. After identifying themselves as DEA agents, Chris said that they had sensitive information that needed to be kept confidential. Patricia nodded. He revealed that Miguel's plan to assassinate Pallomari was in an advanced stage. Unsurprised, Patricia said her husband was hiding for that reason. For a year, she hadn't seen him and didn't know where he was. Dave said that her life was in imminent danger. She shrugged. She would try to relay a message to Pallomari, but it might take a few days. Frustrated by her nonchalance, he said that she was being shadowed by cartel members out to assassinate her husband. After leaving, the agents shared their dismay at her lack of interest in such an increasingly dangerous situation.

Later the same day, Yusti told Jorge that he had pinpointed Pallomari's apartment and was going to assassinate him that evening. Jorge told him to wait for verification of Pallomari being home. If there was a botched attempt, Pallomari would flee and never be found. Jorge needed a few days to get the information from the telephone company.

On Wednesday, August 9, Jorge met the agents at the construction site. He updated them on Yusti's intentions. With their options limited, the agents returned to the computer company. Patricia had no news about Pallomari, but she wanted to meet the US ambassador to discuss the legal consequences her husband faced in America.

The same day, the agents met Jorge again at the construction site. While they were discussing what to do, William called Jorge and ranted about the lack of progress with Pallomari. If the accountant wasn't dead by the end of the week, then Jorge would be killed.

Jorge had no choice but to give Yusti the go-ahead. When Yusti arrived to perform the hit, he couldn't get near the building due to police roadblocks, which the agents had arranged. For a few hours, Yusti waited for the police to leave. Eventually, he went home.

In the meantime, Jorge drove his wife to a field with a mountain view, and explained that he was responsible for the arrest of his bosses. The family was in grave danger, but they would all be moved to America within days. For a long time, they'd be unable to return to Colombia. His wife sobbed, and demanded to know why she had been kept in the dark. Jorge said it was for her own safety. After wiping away tears, she said she would go with him wherever he wanted. They spent almost an hour discussing the plan. She wanted to buy luggage cases immediately. Jorge said they would be in trouble if the cartel found out that they were packing to leave.

Contemplating how to get Pallomari out of the country was giving the agents a headache. Due to his crimes, Colombia had jurisdiction, but if he were arrested by the Colombian police, he would be killed immediately because of his knowledge of all of the cartel's money that had gone to the presidential campaign. Pallomari would have to be removed from Colombia surreptitiously.

On Thursday, Patricia showed up at the US embassy. She wanted to know the financial and legal implications of Pallomari moving to the US. During the meeting, Chris's pager vibrated, and he excused himself to call Jorge. Chris learned that Yusti had confirmed Pallomari's presence in the apartment. The hit was going to proceed that evening. Chris returned to the meeting, and announced what he had just heard. Pallomari had to be rescued now otherwise he would be dead by tomorrow.

In the meantime, Jorge's wife went luggage shopping. Figuring that it was unsafe to be seen taking luggage home, she found luggage that she liked and left her telephone number at the store, so that she could collect it on Friday. When she told Jorge, he knew that if the store called his home, William would find out because his phone was tapped. They would all be killed. Jorge drove to the store and advised the proprietor not to call the number because his phone wasn't working. They would collect the luggage on Friday.

Jorge knew that it was only a matter of time before the

suspicion on his two fall guys was redirected at him. It could happen any day. The safety of his own family now superseded his concern for Pallomari, whose life was proving difficult to save.

On Friday, William called Jorge and demanded his presence at the law offices at 3 pm. From the tone of William's voice, Jorge knew that he was running out of time. William must have figured out that Jorge's two fall guys were not at fault, which would have put Jorge at the top of William's suspect list. Contemplating whether to go to the meeting or to flee to the US embassy, he figured he had just enough room for one more bluff. As an insurance policy to take to the meeting, he rigged a large pager full of C-4 explosives. Its five-second timer would enable him to escape if the situation deteriorated. He also took a mini-claymore mine. While Jorge went inside, a friend stayed in a parked car with instructions to call the army if he didn't hear from Jorge.

Seated on a couch in the law offices, Jorge waited in a room full of armed hit men. Having never been asked to wait this long before, he knew he was in trouble. An overweight hit man in an orange shirt sitting next to him had a .357 Magnum tucked into his waistband. Flicking through a magazine, another hit man was commenting on pornography. Jorge viewed the new generation of assassins as a sign of the cartel's deterioration.

Finally, Jorge was asked to enter the inner chamber, where William was sitting in a swivel chair behind a desk. At the desk were a Search Bloc captain and a hit man called the Shadow. Jorge greeted the captain, who responded coldly. Without knocking, Jorge's second-in-command, Dario, entered. His access to the room meant that he had been promoted and was no longer a suspected informant.

Tilted back in his chair and steepling his fingertips, William asked Jorge if he were involved in any other projects besides Pallomari. Jorge said no. His offer of further assistance was cut short by William, who announced that Dario was taking over Jorge's Pallomari duties. William asked what else Jorge had been up to. Jorge demanded recognition for the people working under him. They needed new assignments and their families taken care of. William said Dario was in charge of that.

Jorge's pager vibrated. He asked William to excuse him, so that he could call Yusti. Jorge grabbed a phone and dialled. Yusti said that everything would be completed that night. To get through the police roadblocks, he had procured documents from a friend who worked at the prosecutor's office. Jorge told him to be careful. To not get caught with fake documents. Yusti boasted that the documents were real, and that the work was going to be done just after 1 am, with an actual arrest warrant from the prosecutor's office.

After hanging up, Jorge reported the update to William, whose face crinkled as if he were displeased that Jorge was still involved with Pallomari. Jorge felt that William hadn't quite figured out what to do with him. Taking advantage of William's indecision, Jorge said that he needed to return home. Fearful that William would prevent him from leaving, Jorge was mindful of the explosives he was carrying as he walked towards the door. Nobody stopped him.

Jorge expected William to add him to the hit list before the attempt on Pallomari's life. At his storage space, he took stock of his many guns and explosives. He grabbed a rifle, a submachinegun, hand grenades and ammunition, which he hid under his bed. He lived in a secure apartment building, and a neighbour, a Supreme Court judge, had around-the-clock armed guards, whom Jorge hoped would deter any lone assassins such as Yusti.

Unfortunately, the same residential complex housed the mother of Freckles, a cartel hit man on friendly terms with the building's security guards, to whom he paid big tips. If dispatched to kill Jorge, Freckles could easily access the building. Freckles' many cartel missions over the years included killing his own brother and the bombing of Pablo Escobar's Monaco building.

The greatest threat to Jorge's safety came from the authorities operating for the cartel. If a prosecutor or the police attempted to arrest him, he would have to use the full force of his weaponry, otherwise he would end up captured and killed in police custody.

Jorge relayed Yusti's plan to the agents. Hoping to convince Pallomari that a DEA safe house was his best option, Chris and Dave flew to Cali with four agents in an eight-passenger plane. They brought the DEA ID of an absent colleague for Pallomari's use.

Patricia had arranged for Pallomari to meet the agents at 11 pm on the night of his scheduled assassination. The meeting spot was outside a busy hospital, where everyone would blend into the crowd. Chris and Dave stood in an obvious place, while the other agents hid.

At 10:45 pm, Pallomari, Patricia and their two boys arrived carrying luggage. Chris reassured the terrified family that the agents would help them. Presently, they only had room on the plane to take Pallomari, so Patricia and the children needed to fly to Bogotá on a regular plane the next morning. Pallomari said goodbye to his family, and got in the back of a car with Chris and Dave. Another car went ahead in case of police roadblocks as even the DEA feared the authorities.

At 2:30 am, Jorge was sleeping with a submachinegun when his phone rang. Dario asked if he had heard from Yusti. Jorge said no and asked why. Unable to find Yusti, Dario said that he had been scheduled to meet the hit man at 2 am, but he hadn't shown up. Jorge told him to wait it out, and that he was going back to bed.

At 6 am, the phone rang. Dario asked Jorge to guess what had happened. Having no idea, Jorge was told that Yusti had been shot in the head while sitting in his car. Due to the professionalism of the hit, cartel members were looking for someone to blame, and suspicion had fallen on Dario, who was worried he would be next. Jorge said that no one would believe such rumours. Dario said the funeral was on Sunday. Jorge pledged to attend. After the call, Jorge tried to decipher what had happened to Yusti. Maybe Yusti wasn't dead, and it was a trap or maybe the CIA had intervened as part of the Pallomari operation.

At 9 am on Saturday, Jorge spoke to the agents, who had secured Pallomari, and were about to pick up his family at the airport. Upon hearing about the death of Yusti, they were surprised. Dave joked that an angel had performed the hit. After laughing, Jorge pretended to take credit by stating that he couldn't allow anything bad to happen. Dave fell silent as if believing the claim. With his family ready to leave, Jorge wanted to know what time the DEA was going to pick them up. When the agents said Monday, Jorge almost fell over. His family would be endangered for two more days. Struggling to stay calm, he asked if it could be sooner. The agents said they were occupied with Pallomari. After getting off the phone, Jorge told his wife that they had two more days to wait. He barricaded the front door and prayed.

At the Bogotá airport, the agents met Pallomari's wife and sons. Patricia said that she wanted to leave her sons in Bogotá and return to Cali until midweek because she had some business to finalise, including selling furniture. Flabbergasted, Chris asked whether the furniture was worth her life. For an hour, the agents tried to change her mind. Dave said that she was foolish and suicidal. Without any power to detain her, the exasperated agents had to let her go. They gave her an emergency phone number for a rescue team. The agents took the two boys to Pallomari's safe house in Bogotá. After hearing about his wife's decision, he sobbed and punched and head-butted the wall. He swore he would not leave the country without her.

While his family watched TV, Jorge positioned himself near a window with a view of the apartment building's entrance. For two days, he monitored the area for hit men such as Freckles. By Monday, the family had packed all of their luggage. If someone from the cartel were to show up while they were transporting the luggage, William would know why they were fleeing and order their execution. To prevent that, a friend in Jorge's van was going to transport the luggage to Bogotá.

Jorge drove to his storage space, removed all of the weapons and took them to a remote location. He buried twenty rifles and boxes of explosives and ammunition. He was going to tell the agents the location, so that they could get them later. As a final means of protection, he kept a submachinegun and a pistol, which he hoped he would need for only a few more hours. Heading back to collect his family, Jorge zigzagged across Cali to avoid getting followed.

The family was scheduled to arrive at an airbase at 1 pm to catch a 2 pm flight to Bogotá. They were having their final meal at the apartment when the phone rang. In a brotherly tone, Freckles greeted Jorge. They needed to talk. He wanted to know where they could meet. As he was having lunch, Jorge offered to meet at Freckle's place at 2 pm. That was fine for Freckles, who hung up. Jorge assumed that Freckles had called to confirm his whereabouts. The proposed meeting was probably a ruse. Freckles could have them under surveillance already. He may have even called from his mother's apartment. Now that the cartel knew exactly where Jorge was, William may have dispatched other hit men.

With his pulse rising, Jorge told his family that it was time to leave. They all got into his car. Armed with a submachinegun, Jorge drove with one hand. His cartel pager started beeping, but he ignored it. To avoid any run-ins with the authorities, he drove at the speed limit and kept the gun out of sight next to the driver's-side door.

After snaking across Cali, Jorge arrived at an airbase, where his family was greeted by Chris and Dave. Just before 2:30 pm, they were guided towards a small plane. Jorge's pager was beeping. Holding it up for his wife to see, he turned it off and said it was all over. She beamed.

In Bogotá, the DEA had to take extra precautions against the authorities. The Colombian president was embroiled in the scandal of taking hot money, which Jorge and Pallomari had inside information on, making them both liabilities. If they attempted to leave the country through the regular channels, and ended up detained by officials, it would be in the best interests of the Colombian president to order their assassinations. Unable to locate them, the Colombian government, Jorge assumed, was probably doing everything it possibly could to prevent the DEA from putting them on a flight to America. The longer they were in the country, the more chance that assassins from the government or the cartel would get the job done. Jorge and Pallomari were the two most wanted men in Colombia. Between hit men looking to impress William, and corrupt police and politicians, Jorge estimated that there were probably over 1,000 people in Bogotá attempting to track him down.

The agents put Jorge and his family into a five-bedroom penthouse apartment used by a US embassy official who was out of the country. Although the penthouse had multiple extra locks on its doors, Jorge feared that it was an easy target for the cartel or the government. Further delaying their evacuation, Jorge and his family could not leave until all of their travel documents were finalised.

As the cartel was unable to get Jorge, reprisals would fall on his parents. His 78-year-old father, an ex-army general, didn't want to leave his home in Bogotá in the country that he had bravely defended until Jorge convinced him that it was too dangerous to stay. The ex-general and his wife were guaranteed that they could eventually return to Colombia when things were safer.

By Wednesday, Patricia had not arrived in Bogotá as scheduled. Her housekeeper told Pallomari that when she had left in the morning everything had been fine. Then a disturbing voicemail had arrived stating that they knew what she was doing. Patricia's suitcases were still by the front door. Further enquiries revealed that Patricia and a colleague had left work at 7:30 pm in his car. No one had seen them after that.

While Jorge waited, the agents showed up on Wednesday night. Chris asked Jorge what would happen if Pallomari's wife went back to Cali. Jorge said she that she would be killed, so the agents must not allow her to go. Chris said she had already left. In that case, Jorge said, she was dead.

In shock, Pallomari abandoned security protocol by making

calls to Cali from his safe house in Bogotá, calls that could have been traced to expose his location. One of Gilberto's hit men told him that Patricia had been kidnapped because Pallomari had disobeyed Gilberto's orders. They would release her if Pallomari refused to cooperate with the DEA and he returned to Cali.

Assuming that if he did as instructed, he would be killed and that Patricia was already dead, Pallomari decided to leave the country. Dealing with the bureaucracy of the DEA was taking too much time, so he chartered a private flight to Florida, where he entered the Federal Witness Protection Program with his sons.

During debriefing, Pallomari told the DEA agents that he had lived for six months in terror of his entire family getting tortured and slaughtered. One of the cartel members he feared the most was a man whom he had seen outside his window, no doubt thinking up ways to kill him. He identified the man as the cartel's head of security: Jorge.

Not wanting to disclose the nature of Jorge's role, Chris told Pallomari that they would revisit that subject. Eventually, Chris asked Pallomari why he was there. The accountant said that the agents had saved him. Chris said no, Jorge had saved him. They detailed the main things that Jorge had done such as organising the roadblocks to prevent Yusti from accessing Pallomari's building.

On December 15, 1998, Pallomari pleaded guilty to conspiracy, racketeering and money laundering charges. Cooperating with the government, he became the world's most important witness of international drug trafficking. He detailed how drug money was paid to politicians, and how corrupt the entire system was. His testimony led to hundreds of people losing their jobs in Colombia, ranging from politicians to the police. Pallomari served a short sentence, and was released to a safe house, where he lived under a fake name.

A few days after Pallomari had fled the country, Colombian Federal police raided Jorge's parents' home in the hope of tracking him down, so he could be disappeared. If he got to the United

States, his testimony would seriously damage the credibility of the Colombian president, not to mention all of the other officials in politics, the police and the army whose cosy relationships with the cartel Jorge could detail.

Jorge's family took two separate flights to Florida. The DEA feared that the airport authorities would arrest Jorge, so the agents applied for a special clearance to fly him out of the country.

On his own, Jorge's paranoia increased. Knowing that the cartel had wiretapped US embassy numbers, he tried to avoid the phone. Expecting a call from his family in America, he answered, but it was a female who insisted on taking a survey. Jorge tried to dismiss her, but she wouldn't hang up. Worried it was an attempt by the cartel to locate him, he demanded to be moved, but Chris and Dave were in America. His new guardians refused to relocate him.

Jorge told the DEA that he was no longer safe there. He was going to move out on his own that night. The DEA backed down, and found him a hideout. He had been in such a rush to move that the new place had not been cleaned. He found empty leftover food, boxes, cups and plates. Throwing everything into a trash bag, he noticed a picture of a woman drawn by a child. From the long hair and dark eyes, he knew it was Patricia. The DEA had put him in the safe house that Pallomari had compromised by calling Cali. After struggling not to think about Patricia's corpse gazing at him through a plastic sheet, Jorge considered his predicament, flabbergasted by the lapse in security. The safe house was probably already under cartel surveillance. He demanded to be moved, but was told he had to wait until Saturday.

On Saturday, two black SUVs arrived with numerous armed agents. Jorge was told to get onto the floor of one. Unable to see anything, he was thrown around by the vehicle's twists and turns. Eventually, the SUVs parked inside the US embassy's walled compound.

The DEA attaché commended Jorge – the most wanted man in Colombia – for his bravery. He thanked Jorge on behalf of the

American public. With so many people looking to kill Jorge, it was necessary to get him out of the country immediately without the knowledge of the Colombian government.

With the SUVs heading for a US government hangar at the Bogotá airport, Jorge was instructed to remain on the floor and to keep his head down. When the bumpy ride was over, the SUVs drove into the hangar. When the hangar's doors were shut, Jorge was allowed out of the SUV. He was escorted onto a small plane. Being the only passenger, he took the seat nearest to the cockpit.

With the hangar's doors still closed, the pilot started the plane and radioed for permission to take off. After clearance, the hangar's doors opened. Within minutes, the plane was airborne. Jorge admired the view of the mountains and the jungle. He wondered what his new life would be like in America. The DEA had promised him over $1 million in reward money and US citizenship for his entire family.

After learning that Jorge had left the country, the Cali Cartel offered $2 million to anyone who could provide his American address.

CHAPTER 14
DEMISE

Even though Gilberto, Miguel and William had managed to keep the cartel going, their rivals were eager to take advantage of their troubles.

Following his arrest in the restaurant, Chepe served six months in a maximum-security prison. In January 1996, a team of prosecutors arrived in the morning to question him. At midday, they left. In the afternoon, a vehicle arrived with a team of interrogators, who were going to continue the questioning. Instead of interrogating him, they smuggled him out of the prison. By hiring a fake team of interrogators, Chepe had escaped.

The authorities searched Bogotá and Cali, but found no clues of his whereabouts. The Colombian government offered $2 million for information leading to his arrest. It was rumoured that he was forming an alliance with FARC guerrillas.

In August 1996, Chepe's bullet-riddled corpse was found. The official report stated that he had died on August 5 in a shootout with the police who had set up an ambush. It omitted that his corpse showed signs of torture. US investigators suspected rival traffickers.

Chepe's family demanded a second autopsy. Their lawyer accused the police of converting deterrent orders into execution orders. Refusing a second autopsy, General Serrano defended the expertise and professionalism of the first. He added that Chepe's family's lawyer "should not be exercising his profession with the background he has."

In May 1996, William was eating lunch at a Brazilian restaurant, surrounded by bodyguards and associates such as Dario. At 1:30 pm, assassins shot the two lookouts William had posted outside. Before William's group could respond, a dozen hit men opened fire with machine guns. Within seconds, William and his men were floored. With the job done – all of the targets seemed dead – the rivals fled.

As soon as they had left, William managed to stand. Although shot in the stomach, he had survived thanks to a bodyguard who had absorbed gunfire meant for him. In hospital, doctors saved his life.

Six people had died, including three of William's closest friends. Meeting their mothers and telling them that it was his fault that their sons had died was a turning point in his life. His role in the cartel had been driven by hunger for power. The close call with death and the loss of his friends made him realise that the price of that lifestyle was too high. He wanted out.

Six weeks later, William limped into a pizzeria surrounded by bodyguards. By coincidence, Chris and Dave were eating there. Recognising William, Chris said that he was going to say hello. Before Dave could object, Chris approached the table. Dave's hand reached for his gun.

Chris said that he was glad William was feeling better. The traffickers smiled. Chris pointed at Dave. William waved at Dave, who couldn't wave back because his hands were under the table clutching his weapon. Chris offered to help William with medical treatment in America. He could arrange a medical visa. Aware that entering America would get him arrested, William thanked Chris, but declined.

In 2006, after over a decade on the run, William surrendered to US agents in Panama. His lawyer claimed that he had serious health issues and feared for his life. Charged with money laundering and bribery, he agreed to cooperate to obtain a lesser sentence. In Miami, he appeared in court in ankle chains, blue jeans and a blue shirt. The balding 40-year-old was sentenced to 21 years. To get his sentence down took a big bribe. Giving the US authorities over $1 billion in assets reduced his sentence to 8 years. The authorities cited William's good behaviour for his early release in 2010.

In 2014, William published a book in Spanish called *I Am the Son of the Cali Cartel* by William Rodriguez Abadia. He does interviews and can be found on Twitter @William_RoAb

By January 1997, Gilberto and Miguel had managed to whittle down the maximum sentence of 24 years that they were facing. Gilberto signed a plea bargain for 10½ years, and Miguel for 9. The DEA complained about the leniency and pressured the Colombian government to add more time by using the brothers' pending cases. In February 1997, Miguel refused to take responsibility for a charge of shipping 330 pounds of cocaine to Florida. Found guilty, he received 23 years from a judge who had refused a $1 million bribe.

While maintaining pressure on the Colombian government to extradite the godfathers, the US authorities went after the cartel's assets and money. The godfathers had funnelled billions into legitimate companies, including those that produced and sold pharmaceutical drugs. By obtaining public documents, the US authorities exposed the godfathers' corporate holdings. The godfathers attempted to transfer the holdings to family members, which only stalled the seizure of the companies.

When it came to bribing judges, the Chess Player had better luck than his brother. On November 7, 2002, a judge ordered Gilberto's early release. The news shocked Colombia and surprised the DEA and the Colombian president. After six years of incarceration, Gilberto was free. Four months later, he was charged with conspiring to import 330 pounds of cocaine into America in 1990 and promptly rearrested.

The business foundation of the Cali Cartel was still the Drogas de Rebaja drugstores that Pablo had targeted with bombs. The Colombian government succeeded where Pablo had failed. It seized 400 drugstores in 26 cities in September 2004. The operation involved approximately 450 prosecutors and 4,000 police.

It was considered the most important seizure of Mafia assets in Colombia's history.

The Cali godfathers incarcerated in Colombia had a choice of quitting the business and not getting extradited. Instead, they converted their prison cells into offices and continued to run the illegal business. When Colombia restored its extradition treaty in 1997, the godfathers should have retired from cocaine. Choosing to commit crimes after 1997 made them eligible for extradition. The DEA finally got what it wanted when the brothers extraditions were approved.

On December 3, 2004, an armoured vehicle transported Gilberto – snowy haired and clean shaved – to a military base, where he was allowed one last call in Colombia. With a bullet-proof vest over a brown jacket, Gilberto was escorted by 120 troops in military vehicles and a helicopter. The DEA took custody of him at the airport.

In the USA, the brothers agreed to 30-year sentences and to forfeit over $2 billion in exchange for immunity from prosecution for almost 30 of their family members, including spouses, children, nephews and nieces. Threatening to indict family members is a common strategy used by the DEA. Chained at the ankles and dressed in dark suits, the godfathers shuffled into a federal courtroom on September 26, 2006.

"I'm willingly submitting myself to American justice," Gilberto said.

"I want to apologise to my family," Miguel said, "and ask for forgiveness for any sufferings I may have caused them. I'm doing this fully convinced it will bring something better."

After sentencing, the prosecutors held a press conference: "The brothers' guilty pleas effectively signal the final fatal blow to the powerful Cali Cartel… There are always other traffickers and thus continuing challenges for law enforcement, but this is a day of pride for the people of Colombia and for international law enforcement."

Seventy-eight-year-old Gilberto is housed at the Federal

Correctional Institution Butner in North Carolina. If he ever wants to see freedom, he will have to live into his nineties. Miguel is incarcerated at the Federal Correctional Institution Edgefield in South Carolina. His release is scheduled for 2030, when he will be 87.

This book started with the fourth and youngest godfather, Pacho, playing soccer, which was the last thing he did before he died. On November 4, 1998, Pacho, 47, was on a soccer pitch at a prison near his hometown, Palmira.

On September 1, 1996, Pacho had surrendered to General Serrano. At the Search Bloc's Cali headquarters, Pacho had arrived in a purple tailored double-breasted suit, a pink and lilac silk tie, a white shirt and aviator glasses with a pink tint. With his thick dark hair greased back, he appeared to have stepped off a catwalk.

Questioned by the DEA, Pacho was cordial, while withholding valuable information. Eventually, he did cooperate to obtain leniency. He provided information about 35 cartel members, including some of his own family. Initially, he was sentenced to 6 years and 8 months for drug trafficking and ordered to pay a $1 million fine.

Believing that he had used his influence with corrupt officials, the DEA criticised the light sentence. The agency wanted him extradited for his role in directing cocaine distribution and money laundering in New York. In 1996, the US Attorney General asked Colombia to extradite Pacho, but because he had turned himself in prior to 1997, the extradition law didn't apply. In 1998, Pacho's sentence was increased to 14 years in response to US pressure.

Although classified as a maximum-security inmate, Pacho had free reign of the prison. He met his lawyers and others in various parts of the complex. He commenced a bachelor's degree in business administration. As the prison's sports organiser, he channelled his energy into soccer and he sponsored tournaments.

On November 4, 1998, one of Pacho's most frequent visitors, Uribe, showed up at the prison gates posing as a lawyer. Upon seeing Uribe approaching, Pacho halted the soccer game to greet his personal adviser. After they had hugged, Uribe pulled out a gun and aimed it at Pacho. He fired six shots into Pacho's head and stomach. He died in hospital.

Inmates grabbed Uribe and handed him over to the guards. Uribe claimed that he had killed Pacho for threatening his family. The threats had supposedly arisen because Uribe had failed to kill one of Pacho's enemies. But Uribe had manufactured the motive to protect the rival Norte del Valle Cartel, who had sanctioned the hit to capture business from Cali's decline.

As *Narcos* puts it, no matter who ends up in charge, "The blow must go on."

CHAPTER 15
WAR ON DRUGS CONCLUSION

When a cartel is dismantled, crime rises as other traffickers compete violently to take its place, hence the murders of Chepe and Pacho. With so much profit in cocaine, the demise of the Cali Cartel did nothing to stop the cocaine entering America.

"Economics has a natural law," Gilberto said. "Supply is determined by demand. When cocaine stops being consumed, when there's no demand for it… that will be the end of that business."

Every year, the black market created by US drug laws expands, the traffickers make greater profits and more money is allocated to fighting the War on Drugs. These sums are so astronomical that both sides have a vested interest in the continuation of prohibition. Over $1 trillion from US taxpayers alone has been funnelled into the War on Drugs. It's a feeding trough for parasitic entities, ranging from private prisons to the manufacturers of the guns that the troops and traffickers point at each other.

Countries like Colombia receive billions of dollars in aid from America provided their governments do what America wants, including fighting the War on Drugs. These governments know that the War on Drugs is a hoax on the taxpayers, and they are keen to participate in the charade. To ensure the flow of aid, foreign governments in partnership with the traffickers stage arrests and drugs' seizures. After the media and photographers leave, the drugs are sold on the black market because drug money is just as enticing to politicians as US taxpayers' dollars. To show the US how well they are fighting the War on Drugs, foreign governments fill their jails with low level smugglers, dealers and users, while working with the bigger players like they did for decades with the Cali Cartel.

Drug laws purport to improve the well-being of society, but in reality, they have damaged it immensely. Due to the mass incarceration of low-level drug offenders, America has 25% of the world's prison population, including approximately 220,000 women. US teenagers claim that it is easier for them to obtain heroin than it is alcohol because criminal gangs don't have any qualms about selling drugs to schoolkids. If the government returned the administration of drugs back to doctors – which was the case before prohibition – the black market would cease to exist and the criminals would be out of jobs. A government-controlled market would have barriers to prevent teenagers from accessing drugs such as heroin.

Narcos relies heavily on the perspectives of DEA agents. The DEA is one of the main parasitic entities thriving off the War on Drugs. It was formed in 1973 with an annual budget of $75 million. By 2014, the budget was over $2 billion. The DEA began with 1,470 special agents. Today, it has over 10,000 employees: over 5,000 special agents and over 5,000 support staff. It has over 200 domestic offices in 21 divisions throughout the US and 87 foreign offices in 63 countries. Since the DEA started, millions of jobs have been created in the justice system to process the incarceration of mostly low-level drug users with the highest category being marijuana possession. By 2016, there were 1,315,561 lawyers in America. The government purports to be fighting the kingpins of the world such as Gilberto and Miguel, while the average arrest is a young person possessing a small amount of drugs for personal use. A disproportionate amount of those arrested are black people.

Policing drugs has turned some sections of the DEA into a Mafia. A Justice Department review published in March 2015 found that DEA agents in Colombia were receiving favours from the cartels, including money, gifts, weapons and prostitutes. They attended sex parties financed by cartels, which the Colombian police guarded. The parties were held in quarters leased by the government with US taxpayers' dollars. Accessible at the parties were sensitive paperwork, computers and other government-issued equipment. After having sex, two DEA agents assaulted a prostitute over a money dispute. The punishment the agents received ranged from a letter of caution to getting suspended for two weeks.

Eric Newman, the show-runner for *Narcos*, was asked whether he had any communication with Pablo's family. An opportunity arose for him to speak to Juan Pablo, but it was shut down by the *Narcos'* DEA agents Murphy and Peña. They protested that Pablo's son had been recorded threatening people. He had been present for tortures and murders. He ran the drugs business while Pablo was hiding... Murphy and Peña told Newman that they would not do business with him if he was going to include Juan Pablo. This was an odd reaction seeing as Juan Pablo had appeared in a film called *Sins of My Father*, which featured him meeting some of the children of his father's victims and asking for their forgiveness. Juan Pablo is on a mission of peace. A more likely explanation for their reaction is what *Narcos* left untold about US complicity in drug-trafficking, which the DEA doesn't want the public to know.

For example, the Castaño brothers ended up with some of Pablo's cocaine infrastructure, but unlike the Cali Cartel, they were intentionally not targeted in the War on Drugs. After Pablo's death, Carlos Castaño was rewarded with a trip to Disneyland. Amnesty International claimed that the reward was actually for his work for Los Pepes. As the Castaño brothers continued to wipe out guerrillas and anyone on the political left, they were allowed to traffic cocaine with impunity under CIA protection. With the blessing of the Colombian and American governments, the Castaños' United Self-Defense Forces of Colombia (AUC) – often working with the state security apparatuses – unleashed far more hell than Pablo. The US State Department classified Fidel as "more ferocious than Escobar, has more military capability, and can count on fellow anti-guerrillas in the Colombian Army and Colombian National Police." The Castaño brothers boasted about killing union leaders on behalf of corporations. "We kill trade unionists because they interfere with people working," Carlos Castaño said.

According to the author and lecturer on international politics Doug Stokes, the Wars on Drugs and Terror are used as pretexts in Colombia to justify funding the military, so it can pacify armed groups and unarmed progressive social forces that threaten a status quo that is conducive to US interests. There is a correlation between the maximisation of corporate profits and the murders of union activists, peasants, priests and human rights campaigners. While pretending to fight a War on Drugs, the US has sponsored drug-funded terrorists such as the Castaño brothers, and sprayed massive amounts of crop-killing chemicals on peasant farmers who suffered and died. Creating a refugee crisis, poisoned land drove numerous Colombians to urban slums and garbage dumps. US aid continues to enable the Colombian elites to brutalise the poor and keep many living in misery.

The illegal market in drugs has corrupted every level of government, right up to the intelligence services and the White House. The US government, including the DEA, CIA and Justice Department used Pablo Escobar and the Cali Cartel as scapegoats to hide their complicity in drug-trafficking, which I have detailed in this War on Drugs series, and which Pablo Escobar's son, Juan Pablo, spoke out about earlier this year, stating that Pablo had been working with the CIA in the earlier years.

"In my book," Juan Pablo said, referring to his second book, "I tell the story of my father working for the CIA selling cocaine to finance the fight against Communism in Central America. The drug business is very different than what we dreamed. What the CIA was doing was buying the controls to get the drug into their country and getting a wonderful deal. He [Pablo] did not make the money alone, but with US agencies that allowed him access to this money. He had direct relations with the CIA... The person who sold the most drugs to the CIA was Pablo Escobar... My father was a cog in a big business of universal drug trafficking."

An alliance with Pablo gave the CIA control of the cocaine entering America, which it used to finance illegal covert operations such as a war in Nicaragua. The person in the US federal government with power over this operation was George HW Bush. He was simultaneously purporting to fight a War on Drugs, while facilitating the entry of billions of dollars' worth of cocaine into America, all done with CIA protection. By controlling both sides of the chessboard, billions were made by the corporate interests Bush represented.

In recent years, the damage caused by the War on Drugs has become more apparent, and public opinion has reached an inflection point. People are tired of the lies from politicians, and so many young people, people of colour, women and those with addiction issues – including numerous soldiers with PTSD – getting warehoused in brutal private prisons for possessing small amounts of drugs. As we have seen with the repeal of marijuana prohibition in many states, politicians will be forced to reverse harmful drug laws if enough of us demand it.

GET A FREE BOOK

Sign Up For My Newsletter:

http://shaunattwood.com/newsletter-subscribe/

REFERENCES

Bowden, Mark. *Killing Pablo*. Atlantic Books, 2001.

Bowen, Russell. *The Immaculate Deception*. America West Publishers, 1991.

Chepesiuk, Ron. *Drug Lords: The Rise and Fall of the Cali Cartel*. Milo Books, 2003.

Chepesiuk, Ron. *Escobar vs Cali: The War of the Cartels*. Strategic Media, 2013.

Cockburn, Leslie. *Out of Control*. Bloomsbury, 1988.

Cockburn and Clair. *Whiteout*. Verso, 1998.

Escobar, Juan Pablo. *Pablo Escobar: My Father*. Ebury Press, 2014.

Escobar, Roberto. *Escobar*. Hodder & Stoughton, 2009.

Grillo, Joan. *El Narco*. Bloomsbury, 2012.

Gugliotta and Leen. *Kings of Cocaine*. Harper and Row, 1989.

Hari, Johann. *Chasing the Scream*. Bloomsbury, 2015.

Hopsicker, Daniel. *Barry and the Boys*. MadCow Press, 2001.

Leveritt, Mara. *The Boys on the Tracks*. Bird Call Press, 2007.

Levine, Michael. *The Big White Lie*. Thunder's Mouth Press, 1993.

Marquez, Gabriel Garcia. *News of a Kidnapping*. Penguin, 1996.

Massing, Michael. *The Fix*. Simon & Schuster, 1998.

McAleese, Peter. *No Mean Soldier*. Cassell Military Paperbacks. 2000.

McCoy, Alfred. *The Politics of Heroin in Southeast Asia*. Harper and Row, 1972.

Morris, Roger. *Partners in Power.* Henry Holt, 1996.

Noriega, Manuel. *The Memoirs of Manuel Noriega.* Random House, 1997.

North, Oliver. *Under Fire.* Harper Collins, 1991.

Paley, Dawn. *Drug War Capitalism.* AK Press, 2014.

Porter, Bruce. *Blow.* St Martin's Press, 1993.

Reed, Terry. *Compromised.* Clandestine Publishing, 1995.

Rempel, William. *At the Devil's Table: Inside the Fall of the Cali Cartel, the World's Biggest Crime Syndicate.* Random House, 2011.

Ross, Rick. *Freeway Rick Ross.* Freeway Studios, 2014.

Ruppert, Michael. *Crossing the Rubicon.* New Society Publishers, 2004.

Saviano, Roberto. *Zero Zero Zero.* Penguin Random House UK, 2013.

Schou, Nick. *Kill the Messenger.* Nation Books, 2006.

Shannon, Elaine. *Desperados.* Penguin, 1988.

Stich, Rodney. *Defrauding America* 3rd Ed. Diablo Western Press, 1998.

Stich, Rodney. *Drugging America* 2nd Ed. Silverpeak, 2006.

Stokes, Doug. *America's Other War: Terrorizing Colombia.* Zed Books, 2005.

Stone, Roger. *The Clinton's War on Women.* Skyhorse, 2015.

Stone, Roger. *Jeb and the Bush Crime Family.* Skyhorse, 2016.

Streatfield, Dominic. *Cocaine.* Virgin Publishing, 2001.

Tarpley and Chaitkin. *George Bush.* Progressive Press, 2004.

Tomkins, David. *Dirty Combat.* Mainstream Publishing, 2008.

Valentine, Douglas. *The Strength of the Pack.* Trine Day LLC, 2009.

Woods, Neil. *Good Cop Bad War.* Ebury Press, 2016.

SHAUN'S BOOKS

English Shaun Trilogy
Party Time
Hard Time
Prison Time

War on Drugs Series
Pablo Escobar: Beyond Narcos
American Made: Who Killed Barry Seal? Pablo Escobar or George HW Bush
The Cali Cartel: Beyond Narcos
We Are Being Lied To: The War on Drugs (Expected 2018)

Un–Making a Murderer: The Framing of Steven Avery and Brendan Dassey

Life Lessons

Two Tonys (Expected 2019)
T-Bone (Expected 2022)

SOCIAL-MEDIA LINKS

Email: attwood.shaun@hotmail.co.uk
Blog: Jon's Jail Journal
Website: shaunattwood.com
Twitter: @shaunattwood
YouTube: Shaun Attwood
LinkedIn: Shaun Attwood
Goodreads: Shaun Attwood
Facebook: Shaun Attwood, Jon's Jail Journal, T-Bone
Appreciation Society

I welcome feedback on any of my books.
Thank you for the Amazon reviews!

AMERICAN MADE: WHO KILLED BARRY SEAL? PABLO ESCOBAR OR GEORGE HW BUSH

Chapter 1
Official Story of Barry's Death

While Barry Seal packed his briefcase at his home in Baton Rouge, three Colombian hitmen in a hotel room prepared to kill him.

"Debbie, I'm leaving," Barry said, stood in the living room under a grand chandelier, gazing upstairs for his wife.

With brown permed hair, Debbie appeared in a white floral top and blue pants. "OK. I'll meet you for breakfast if you want," she said, resting a hand on the banister, the other holding a hair brush.

"Right after my jog?"

"You started jogging!"

Barry smiled. "Every morning around my new home," he said, referring to the Salvation Army halfway house a judge had ordered him to stay at from 6 pm every night. "If I can't be rich, I might as well still be pretty," Barry said in a slow and pleasant Louisiana accent.

Resting her elbows on the banister, Debbie beamed. "Well, you're pretty to me, rich or poor."

"Whoo-whee!" Barry yelped, shimmying his hips and shoulders. "I'm way past poor, baby doll!" As he checked his watch, his smile evaporated. "Oh, I've got to go. It's quarter to six."

"I love you," Debbie said.

"I love you, too, Mrs Seal."

As her hefty husband with chunky sideburns walked out, Debbie yelled, "Be careful!"

In a hotel room, the Colombians disguised a machine gun by wrapping clothes around it. Walking briskly in light-coloured suits and clothes, they went downstairs and got in a car. The sun had almost disappeared from the skyline as they drove towards the Salvation Army halfway house.

Cruising along the streets of Baton Rouge in a white Cadillac, Barry was looking forward to the end of his six-month sentence at the halfway house. He'd been told that the Medellín Cartel – run by powerful Colombian drug lords, including Pablo Escobar – had put a $500,000 bounty on his head after his status as an informant had been leaked to the press by the Reagan-Bush administration.

It was dark when Barry arrived at the halfway house. He reversed his car towards a two-storey beige building. He was about to get out when a shadowy figure took him by surprise. Barry squinted at the man next to his Cadillac: a thin Colombian with a moustache and a hostile gaze. The man jumped forward and aimed a gun at Barry.

News Anchor Peter Jennings reported, "He used to smuggle drugs and he got caught and he became one of the government's most valuable informants in the war against cocaine. But last night in Louisiana, Barry Seal's enemies caught up with him and killed him. Tonight, three men are in custody. NBC's Brian Ross reports that Seal was about to testify for the government once again."

"Authorities believe that last night's machine-gun killing," Brian Ross said, "of top drug informant Barry Seal was ordered by drug bosses in Medellín, Colombia, who sent five men to Baton Rouge to kill Seal. Seal's son Barry Jr, one of five children, was restrained by police, who said the gunmen had waited in ambush for Seal at a Salvation Army shelter, where Seal had been sentenced by a federal judge on a drug charge to do community service. Seal was a tough-guy TWA pilot, who got caught smuggling cocaine and became one of the most important and daring undercover operatives, infiltrating the top Colombian drug operations. In a recent interview, Seal said he knew he was risking his life."

A clip of Barry's face was shown in a cockpit wearing sunglasses. "The old saying:" Barry said, "'If you can't stand the heat, don't work in the kitchen.' I can take the pressure."

"It was Seal who posed as a smuggler," Brian Ross said, "and flew into Nicaragua and took these pictures showing Colombian drug dealers and Sandinista officials loading cocaine on his plane."

The Reagan-Bush administration had claimed that Pablo Escobar was on one of the grainy pictures.

"Seal busted up the Colombian connection in the Caribbean country of Turks and Caicos, setting up a payoff meeting on videotape that led to the arrest and conviction of the country's prime minister. And Seal was scheduled to be the key witness against this man, Jorge Ochoa, the top Colombian drug boss now in jail in Spain, about to be extradited to the United States. Authorities say the Ochoa drug organisation was responsible for the bombing of the US embassy in Bogotá last year, the assassination of Colombia's attorney general and now the murder in Louisiana of the man who was perhaps the most important undercover drug informant ever."

The rest of the media followed suit by reporting that Barry had been a government witness against drug traffickers, including Jorge Ochoa and Pablo Escobar of the Medellín Cartel, who had sanctioned the hit. Having refused to go into the Federal Witness Protection Program, Barry had been ambushed outside a Louisiana halfway house and died in a hail of bullets. The media later reported that a three-man Colombian hit team had been caught, convicted and sentenced to life without parole. Case closed.

As I researched Barry's life for my War On Drugs trilogy, the official story fell apart. Barry was deeply involved with powerful people who specialised in assassinations and trafficked drugs and weapons on an international scale. The information that he'd amassed working for them as a pilot had rendered him a liability. He died with George HW Bush's telephone number in his possession. To understand why Barry was killed, it's necessary to examine his life beyond its portrayal in Hollywood and the relationships he forged while working for the CIA.

PABLO ESCOBAR: BEYOND NARCOS

Chapter 1
Early Years

Pablo Escobar was born on a cattle ranch in 1949, the second year of The Violence, a civil war that saw millions of Colombians flee their homes and left hundreds of thousands dead. Slicing people up with machetes was popular and led to a new genre of slaughter methods with ornate names. The Flower Vase Cut began with the severing of the head, arms and legs. The liberated limbs were stuffed down the neck, turning the headless torso into a vase of body parts. A victim stabbed in the neck, who had his tongue pulled out through the gap and hung down his chest was wearing a Colombian Necktie. The turmoil affected nearly every family in Colombia. It accustomed Pablo's generation to extreme violence and the expectancy of a short and brutal life.

Pablo's parents were Abel de Jesús Dari Escobar, a hard-working peasant farmer who traded cows and horses, and Hermilda Gaviria, an elementary-school teacher. As her husband was mostly absent due to work, Hermilda cooked, cleaned and took care of her family. Pablo was the third of seven children.

One day, tiny Pablo wandered away from home. Hermilda found him under a tree, with a stick, playing with a snake.

"See, I'm not hurting you," Pablo said to the snake.

Gazing affectionately, Hermilda knew that Pablo was a sweet boy who loved animals.

The nearest school was so far away that Pablo and his brother, Roberto, had to wake up early. With no means of transportation, it took them an hour to walk there in worn-out shoes.

Rather that wear shoes with holes in them, Pablo decided to go to school barefooted. His teacher sent him home. Humiliated, Pablo told his mother that he needed new shoes to stay in school. As she had no money, she deliberated her options and shoplifted a pair of shoes. At home, she noticed that each shoe was a different size. Disheartened, she confessed to a priest, who advised her to return the shoes and get them on credit.

She bought the shoes and arrived home, exhausted and anxious. With such a large family to feed, she complained about their lack of money.

"Don't worry, mom," Pablo said. "Wait until I grow up. I'll give you everything."

As The Violence between the Conservative and Liberal parties escalated, the family was warned to leave or else risk having their body parts re-assembled into art. But having no safe place to go, and loving the animals, the beautiful countryside adorned with wildflowers, and air that carried a taste of pine and resin from the forest, they chose to stay.

Pablo was seven when the guerrillas entered his village near the town of Rionegro, the Black River. Trembling, he heard machetes hacking the front door and threats of murder. He clung to his mother, who was crying and praying. His father said they would be killed, but at least they could try to save the kids. They hid the kids under mattresses and blankets.

The front door was so strong that the guerrillas eventually gave up trying to break in. Instead, they set fire to it. Wincing and coughing in a house filling with smoke, Pablo's parents braced to die. But soldiers arrived and the guerrillas fled.

With a burning building illuminating the street, the town's survivors were escorted to a schoolhouse. Pablo would never forget the charred bodies and the corpses hanging from the lampposts. Internalized in the terrified child, the horrors of The Violence would re-emerge years later, when he kidnapped, murdered and bombed to maintain his empire.

Growing up with six siblings, Pablo bonded the most with Roberto, who was two years his senior. Roberto was intelligent and had a passion for mathematics, electronics and cycling. Pablo enjoyed watching Roberto construct things such as radios, but rather than join in, he sat around for most of the day as if lost in thought.

Pablo and Roberto were sent from the family's ranch to live with their grandmother in the safety of Medellín, known as the City of the Eternal Spring due to a steady climate averaging around 22.2°C or 72°F. Downtown was a cluster of glass and steel skyscrapers separated by roads lined with trees. The surrounding expanse of houses grew more dilapidated towards the shantytowns, slums and garbage dumps – places crammed with displaced people where gangs of street kids, thieves and pickpockets roamed. The tough residents of Medellín worked hard to get ahead.

Pablo's grandmother was an astute businesswoman who bottled sauces and spices and sold them to supermarkets. Under her loving but stern hand, Pablo and Roberto had to go to church and pray every morning.

Although they loved the weather and the mountainous landscape, the second largest city in Colombia with all of its fast cars and over a million people intimidated the brothers, who were accustomed to the tempo of ranch life. They were delighted when their parents joined them, but their father disliked living in the city, so he returned to the countryside to work on other people's farms. Eventually, the brothers fell in love with Medellín.

The atmosphere at home was heavily religious. They had a figurehead of Jesus with realistic blood. After his mother told him Christ's story, young Pablo was so sad that when lunch was served, he put a piece of meat in his corn cake and took it to the figurehead. "Poor man, who made you bleed? Do you want a little meat?" This act convinced his mother that he was kind and religious. For the rest of his life, Pablo would always try to sleep with an image of Jesus nearby.

Hermilda enchanted Pablo with stories about his grandfather,

Roberto Gaviria, who had smuggled whiskey. With long-range planning and a creative imagination, Roberto the bootlegger had outsmarted everyone, including the authorities. Pablo wanted to emulate his grandfather's success.

Growing up in a suburb of Medellín called Envigado, the kids built carts from wood and raced down hills. They made soccer balls from old clothes wrapped inside of plastic bags, erected makeshift goalposts and played with the other kids in the neighbourhood. It was Pablo's favourite sport. A popular prank was to stick chewing gum on a doorbell, so that it rang continuously.

On the streets of Medellín, some of Pablo's leadership and criminal traits started to emerge. Although the youngest in his group, he'd take the lead. When the police confiscated their soccer ball, he encouraged the group to throw rocks at the patrol car. The police rounded up several of the group and threatened to keep them in jail all day. Only Pablo spoke up to the commander. He told them they hadn't done anything bad. They were tired of the ball being taken and they'd pay to retrieve the ball. Some of the kids in the group ended up in business with Pablo later on.

In his early teens, Pablo was elected president of his school's Council for Student Wellness, which demanded transportation and food for indigent students. He learned about the US meddling in South America for its own advantage, which often increased the suffering of the most poverty-stricken people. He hated that the poor were the biggest victims of violence and injustice.

During this time, he absorbed anti-imperialist phrases which became mantras for the rest of his life. He heard rumours that the CIA had facilitated the assassination of Jorge Eliécer Gaitán, a leftist presidential candidate who had defended workers' rights and promised an equitable land reform. Gaitán's death had ignited The Violence that had threatened Pablo's family.

Pablo started to despise the way that society was structured: a tiny percent of the population owned the majority of the land and wealth, while more than half of Colombians lived in poverty. Determined to prevent that from happening to him, he claimed he would kill himself if he had not made a million pesos by the age of thirty.

According to his brother, Roberto, in his book, *Escobar*, Pablo developed an interest in history, world politics and poetry. At the public library, he read law books. He practised public speaking on student audiences at lunchtime or on the soccer field. Roberto remembers him speaking passionately about becoming the president of Colombia and taking ten percent of the earnings of the richest people to help the poor to build schools and roads. To create jobs, he wanted to encourage Asian manufacturers to build plants in Colombia.

In school, Pablo grew restless. Distrustful of authority figures, he felt more at ease with the street gangs. For money, he experimented with small scams. Believing that school was a waste of time, he dropped out for two years. On the dangerous streets, he refined his techniques and learned to avoid the pitfalls.

Hermilda convinced him to resume his education, so he could get the three grades necessary to graduate. As he adored his mother, he went back to school. But he ended up in constant arguments with his teachers whom he viewed as absurd and foolish. Eventually, he was expelled.

After his mother scolded him, he responded, "Mother, I keep on telling you: I want to be big and I will be. I'm poor, but I'll never die poor. I promise."

By sixteen, Pablo was displaying an extraordinary amount of confidence on the streets. With a comb in his pocket, he often gazed at windows to inspect his reflection. In later years, he imitated the mannerisms of Al Capone and *The Godfather* played by Marlon Brando. His deep thinking was intensified by smoking marijuana. He grew quieter. When asked a question, he generally paused silently before replying. Some wondered whether he was imitating *The Godfather*, but it was a natural trait exacerbated when he was stoned.

Rationalising his banditry as a form of resistance to an oppressive society, he channelled his energy into criminal activity, which ranged from selling fake lottery tickets to assaulting people. With a rifle, he walked into banks and calmly told the staff to empty their safes. With a smile, he chatted to the tellers, while awaiting the cash. Unable to perceive that Pablo had shed his sense of fear, some mistakenly ascribed his bravado to drugs. The results he achieved from his cleverness and farsightedness – including eluding the police – boosted his faith in himself.

A formidable combination of intelligence and street smarts enabled him to rise above his contemporaries, some of whom sought his advice and joined his gang. Those who were nervous or frustrated felt safe in his company. He earned their respect by remaining calm and cheerful in dangerous situations.

One said, "He was like a God, a man with a very powerful aura. When I met him for the first time, it was the most important day of my life."

In *Killing Pablo*, author Mark Bowden described Pablo as an accomplished car thief by age twenty. Drivers were forced out of their cars by his gang and the cars dismantled at chop shops. He dictated orders from home, managing the logistics and collecting the cash.

His gang started stealing new cars, which were impossible to resell if they had been reported as stolen. To get around this, he offered the police bribes. After a year, his relationship with them was so strong that the police chiefs followed his orders. Complaints about him reselling stolen cars were ignored.

Money from selling car parts was used to bribe officials to issue car certificates, so that the stolen cars could be resold without having to be chopped. The officials receiving the complaints about what he was doing were the same ones issuing him the titles for the new cars.

He started a protection racket whereby people paid him to prevent their cars from being stolen.

Always generous with his friends, he gave them stolen cars with clean papers. Those receiving new cars were told to pick them up from the factory. If the factory workers detected the forged paperwork, Pablo's friends told them, "These titles were made by Pablo," which prompted the workers to hand over the keys.

Pablo and his cousin, Gustavo – who *Narcos* portrayed as usually wearing a flat cap – built race cars from stolen parts and entered rallies. Suspected of stealing a red Renault, Pablo was arrested in 1974, but he bribed his way out of a conviction.

Pablo ordered the murders of people who tried to prevent his accumulation of power, including those who denounced him, refused to abide by his rule or declined his bribes. He discovered that murder provided cheap and effective PR. Focussing people on their mortality or that of their families brought their behaviour into line. He killed without remorse, just to increase his reputation and earnings.

Some of the people who owed Pablo money were kidnapped. If the debt wasn't paid by family members or friends, the victim was killed. This enhanced his reputation and helped his business grow in a world of opportunists and cutthroats. He also kidnapped people and held them for ransom.

Diego Echavarría Misas was a powerful industrialist who lived in a remake of a medieval castle. Widely respected in the higher social circles, he yearned to be revered as a philanthropist. But no matter how many schools and hospitals he opened, the poor were not fooled by his attempts to mask his malevolence.

The workers in his textile mills toiled endlessly in cruel conditions for a pittance. He fired hundreds of them in an abusive manner and without a severance pay. Like many wealthy landowners, he expanded his territory by forcefully evicting peasant communities. Attempting to defend their homes, some peasants were imprisoned or murdered. The rest were forced to settle in the slums.

Pablo had heard enough about Echavarría. One day, his kidnapping became news. His family rapidly paid the ransom, but his fate remained a mystery. After six weeks, his body was found in a hole near Pablo's birthplace. He had been tortured, beaten and strangled. The poor celebrated his death.

Although many people believed that Pablo had brought them justice, with no evidence linking him to the crime, he was not charged. On the streets, people stopped to shake his hand or bowed to him in reverence. They began calling him "Doctor Escobar" and "The Doctor."

Roberto has claimed that the early stories of his brother's brutality are untrue accusations made by Pablo's enemies.

Pablo started to apply his organisational skills to contraband, a thriving business in Colombia, a country steeped in corruption. Medellín was known as a hub for smugglers. Those who got caught typically bribed their way free. If they were unable to pay a bribe, the police would usually confiscate their contraband rather than incarcerate them. It was the cost of doing business and customary throughout Colombia.

With numerous police on the payroll of crime bosses, it was hard to differentiate between the police and the criminals. The police not only gave their criminal associates freedom from jail, but they also committed crimes for the gangs, including kidnappings and contract killings. Shootouts sometimes occurred between different police on the payrolls of rival gangs.

The court system was the same. Judges who earned $200 a month could charge up to $30,000 to dismiss a case. Judges who refused were threatened or beaten. Court staff could be bribed to lose files, which was cheaper than paying a judge. If that didn't work, the judge was killed. The court system was considered the softest target in law enforcement, and Pablo would master the art of manipulating it.

Early on, *Narcos* presented Pablo as a boss in the contraband smuggling business, but that was false. He was the underling of a powerful contraband kingpin who specialised in transporting cigarettes, electronics, jewellery and clothing in shipping containers from America, England and Japan. The goods were shipped to Colombia via Panama.

Having met Pablo at a soccer match, the kingpin asked him to be a bodyguard, in the hope of reducing worker theft. He told

Pablo that the way to make money was to protect the merchandise for the guy with the money, and that was him.

Pablo bought the poorly-paid workers seafood and wine. He offered them half of his salary forever to work with him. If they stopped stealing, he'd come back and take care of them in two weeks. The workers agreed and returned the stolen goods they still had.

Specialising in cigarettes, Pablo drove across Colombia in a jeep ahead of half a dozen trucks transporting contraband. Along the way, he paid the necessary bribes to the police. Delighted with Pablo's performance, the kingpin offered him ten percent of the business. Pablo demanded fifty. The kingpin called Pablo crazy. Pablo said it was fair because the kingpin had sometimes lost more than half of the goods. Even after Pablo's fifty percent, the kingpin would still make more money because there would be no theft. The kingpin agreed to forty percent.

Through the contraband business, Pablo became adept at smuggling goods across the country, without paying government taxes and fees. Supervising two convoys a month earned him up to $200,000. He stashed his profits in hiding places in the walls of his home. He installed special electronic doors that only he could open. He recruited Roberto as an accountant, in charge of handling the payroll, making investments and depositing money into bank accounts with fake names. Over the years, money was invested in real estate, construction businesses and farms. As his brother was handling so much money, Pablo gave him a gun.

Giving half of his salary to the workers earned their respect and the name El Patrón or the Boss. He bought his mother a house, a taxicab for Gustavo and an Italian bicycle for his brother. He donated truckloads of food to the scavengers at the garbage dumps. He took about twenty members of his family to Disney World in Florida, where he went on all of the rides with his son.

When a policeman on Pablo's payroll was moved to another district, he snitched out the operation. The police waited to ambush a convoy of trucks. They would all get rich confiscating so many goods. Pablo had stopped for lunch and told the convoy to continue without him. Thirty-seven trucks were seized. A driver called Pablo who said to tell the other drivers not to speak to the police. With the police after him, he took a bus back to Medellín. Lawyers got the drivers released but were unable to retrieve the merchandise.

Even though his contraband partnership with the kingpin was over, Pablo soon found a more lucrative business opportunity.

SHAUN ATTWOOD'S TRUE-LIFE JAIL EXPERIENCE

Hard Time New Edition
Chapter 1

Sleep deprived and scanning for danger, I enter a dark cell on the second floor of the maximum-security Madison Street jail in Phoenix, Arizona, where guards and gang members are murdering prisoners. Behind me, the metal door slams heavily. Light slants into the cell through oblong gaps in the door, illuminating a prisoner cocooned in a white sheet, snoring lightly on the top bunk about two thirds of the way up the back wall. Relieved there is no immediate threat, I place my mattress on the grimy floor. Desperate to rest, I notice movement on the cement-block walls. *Am I hallucinating?* I blink several times. The walls appear to ripple. Stepping closer, I see the walls are alive with insects. I flinch. So many are swarming, I wonder if they're a colony of ants on the move. To get a better look, I put my eyes right up to them. They are mostly the size of almonds and have antennae. American cockroaches. I've seen them in the holding cells downstairs in smaller numbers, but nothing like this. A chill spread over my body. I back away.

Something alive falls from the ceiling and bounces off the base of my neck. I jump. With my night vision improving, I spot cockroaches weaving in and out of the base of the fluorescent strip light. Every so often one drops onto the concrete and resumes crawling. Examining the bottom bunk, I realise why my cellmate is sleeping at a higher elevation: cockroaches are pouring from gaps in the decrepit wall at the level of my bunk. The area is thick with them. Placing my mattress on the bottom bunk scatters them. I walk towards the toilet, crunching a few under my shower sandals. I urinate and grab the toilet roll. A cockroach darts from the centre of the roll onto my hand, tickling my fingers. My arm jerks as if it has a mind of its own, losing the cockroach and the toilet roll. Using a towel, I wipe the bulk of them off the bottom bunk, stopping only to shake the odd one off my hand. I unroll my mattress. They begin to regroup and inhabit my mattress. My adrenaline is pumping so much, I lose my fatigue.

Nauseated, I sit on a tiny metal stool bolted to the wall. *How will I sleep? How's my cellmate sleeping through the infestation and my arrival?* Copying his technique, I cocoon myself in a sheet and lie down, crushing more cockroaches. The only way they can access me now is through the breathing hole I've left in the sheet by the lower half of my face. Inhaling their strange musty odour, I close my eyes. I can't sleep. I feel them crawling on the sheet around my feet. *Am I imagining things?* Frightened of them infiltrating my breathing hole, I keep opening my eyes. Cramps cause me to rotate onto my other side. Facing the wall, I'm repulsed by so many of them just inches away. I return to my original side.

The sheet traps the heat of the Sonoran Desert to my body, soaking me in sweat. Sweat tickles my body, tricking my mind into thinking the cockroaches are infiltrating and crawling on me. The trapped heat aggravates my bleeding skin infections and bedsores. I want to scratch myself, but I know better. The outer layers of my skin have turned soggy from sweating constantly in this concrete oven. Squirming on the bunk fails to stop the relentless itchiness of my skin. Eventually, I scratch myself. Clumps of moist skin detach under my nails. Every now and then I become so uncomfortable, I must open my cocoon to waft the heat out, which allows the cockroaches in. It takes hours to drift to sleep. I only manage a few hours. I awake stuck to the soaked sheet, disgusted by the cockroach carcasses compressed against the mattress.

The cockroaches plague my new home until dawn appears

at the dots in the metal grid over a begrimed strip of four-inch-thick bullet-proof glass at the top of the back wall – the cell's only source of outdoor light. They disappear into the cracks in the walls, like vampire mist retreating from sunlight. But not all of them. There were so many on the night shift that even their vastly reduced number is too many to dispose of. And they act like they know it. They roam around my feet with attitude, as if to make it clear that I'm trespassing on their turf.

My next set of challenges will arise not from the insect world, but from my neighbours. I'm the new arrival, subject to scrutiny about my charges just like when I'd run into the Aryan Brotherhood prison gang on my first day at the medium-security Towers jail a year ago. I wish my cellmate would wake up, brief me on the mood of the locals and introduce me to the head of the white gang. No such luck. Chow is announced over a speaker system in a crackly robotic voice, but he doesn't stir.

I emerge into the day room for breakfast. Prisoners in black-and-white bee-striped uniforms gather under the metal-grid stairs and tip dead cockroaches into a trash bin from plastic peanut-butter containers they'd set as traps during the night. All eyes are on me in the chow line. Watching who sits where, I hold my head up, put on a solid stare and pretend to be as at home in this environment as the cockroaches. It's all an act. I'm lonely and afraid. I loathe having to explain myself to the head of the white race, who I assume is the toughest murderer. I've been in jail long enough to know that taking my breakfast to my cell will imply that I have something to hide.

The gang punishes criminals with certain charges. The most serious are sex offenders, who are KOS: Kill On Sight. Other charges are punishable by SOS – Smash On Sight – such as drive-by shootings because women and kids sometimes get killed. It's called convict justice. Gang members are constantly looking for people to beat up because that's how they earn their reputations and tattoos. The most serious acts of violence earn the highest-ranking tattoos. To be a full gang member requires murder. I've observed the body language and techniques inmates trying to integrate employ. An inmate with a spring in his step and an air of confidence is likely to be accepted. A person who avoids eye contact and fails to introduce himself to the gang is likely to be preyed on. Some of the failed attempts I saw ended up with heads getting cracked against toilets, a sound I've grown familiar with. I've seen prisoners being extracted on stretchers who looked dead – one had yellow fluid leaking from his head. The constant violence gives me nightmares, but the reality is that I put myself in here, so I force myself to accept it as a part of my punishment.

It's time to apply my knowledge. With a self-assured stride, I take my breakfast bag to the table of white inmates covered in neo-Nazi tattoos, allowing them to question me.

"Mind if I sit with you guys?" I ask, glad exhaustion has deepened my voice.

"These seats are taken. But you can stand at the corner of the table."

The man who answered is probably the head of the gang. I size him up. Cropped brown hair. A dangerous glint in Nordic-blue eyes. Tiny pupils that suggest he's on heroin. Weightlifter-type veins bulging from a sturdy neck. Political ink on arms crisscrossed with scars. About the same age as me, thirty-three.

"Thanks. I'm Shaun from England." I volunteer my origin to show I'm different from them but not in a way that might get me smashed.

"I'm Bullet, the head of the whites." He offers me his fist to bump. "Where you roll in from, wood?"

Addressing me as wood is a good sign. It's what white gang members on a friendly basis call each other.

"Towers jail. They increased my bond and re-classified me to maximum security."

"What's your bond at?"

"I've got two $750,000 bonds," I say in a monotone. This is no place to brag about bonds.

"How many people you kill, brother?" His eyes drill into mine, checking whether my body language supports my story. My body language so far is spot on.

"None. I threw rave parties. They got us talking about drugs on wiretaps." Discussing drugs on the phone does not warrant a $1.5 million bond. I know and beat him to his next question. "Here's my charges." I show him my charge sheet, which includes conspiracy and leading a crime syndicate – both from running an Ecstasy ring.

Bullet snatches the paper and scrutinises it. Attempting to pre-empt his verdict, the other whites study his face. On edge, I wait for him to respond. Whatever he says next will determine whether I'll be accepted or victimised.

"Are you some kind of jailhouse attorney?" Bullet asks. "I want someone to read through my case paperwork." During our few minutes of conversation, Bullet has seen through my act and concluded that I'm educated – a possible resource to him.

I appreciate that he'll accept me if I take the time to read his case. "I'm no jailhouse attorney, but I'll look through it and help you however I can."

"Good. I'll stop by your cell later on, wood."

After breakfast, I seal as many of the cracks in the walls as I can with toothpaste. The cell smells minty, but the cockroaches still find their way in. Their day shift appears to be collecting information on the brown paper bags under my bunk, containing a few items of food that I purchased from the commissary; bags that I tied off with rubber bands in the hope of keeping the cockroaches out. Relentlessly, the cockroaches explore the bags for entry points, pausing over and probing the most worn and vulnerable regions. *Will the nightly swarm eat right through the paper?* I read all morning, wondering whether my cellmate has died in his cocoon, his occasional breathing sounds reassuring me.

Bullet stops by late afternoon and drops his case paperwork off. He's been charged with Class 3 felonies and less, not serious crimes, but is facing a double-digit sentence because of his prior convictions and Security Threat Group status in the prison system. The proposed sentencing range seems disproportionate. I'll advise him to reject the plea bargain – on the assumption he already knows to do so, but is just seeking the comfort of a second opinion, like many un-sentenced inmates. When he returns for his paperwork, our conversation disturbs my cellmate – the cocoon shuffles – so we go upstairs to his cell. I tell Bullet what I think. He is excitable, a different man from earlier, his pupils almost non-existent.

"This case ain't shit. But my prosecutor knows I done other shit, all kinds of heavy shit, but can't prove it. I'd do anything to get that sorry bitch off my fucking ass. She's asking for something bad to happen to her. Man, if I ever get bonded out, I'm gonna chop that bitch into pieces. Kill her slowly though. Like to work her over with a blowtorch."

Such talk can get us both charged with conspiring to murder a prosecutor, so I try to steer him elsewhere. "It's crazy how they can catch you doing one thing, yet try to sentence you for all of the things they think you've ever done."

"Done plenty. Shot some dude in the stomach once. Rolled him up in a blanket and threw him in a dumpster."

Discussing past murders is as unsettling as future ones. "So, what's all your tattoos mean, Bullet? Like that eagle on your chest?"

"Why you wanna know?" Bullet's eyes probe mine.

My eyes hold their ground. "Just curious."

"It's a war bird. The AB patch."

"AB patch?"

"What the Aryan Brotherhood gives you when you've put enough work in."

"How long does it take to earn a patch?"

"Depends how quickly you put your work in. You have to earn your lightning bolts first."

"Why you got red and black lightning bolts?"

"You get SS bolts for beating someone down or for being an

enforcer for the family. Red lightning bolts for killing someone. I was sent down as a youngster. They gave me steel and told me who to handle and I handled it. You don't ask questions. You just get blood on your steel. Dudes who get these tats without putting work in are told to cover them up or leave the yard."

"What if they refuse?"

"They're held down and we carve the ink off them."

Imagining them carving a chunk of flesh to remove a tattoo, I cringe. He's really enjoying telling me this now. His volatile nature is clear and frightening. *He's accepted me too much. He's trying to impress me before making demands.*

At night, I'm unable to sleep. Cocooned in heat, surrounded by cockroaches, I hear the swamp-cooler vent – a metal grid at the top of a wall – hissing out tepid air. Giving up on sleep, I put my earphones on and tune into National Public Radio. Listening to a Vivaldi violin concerto, I close my eyes and press my tailbone down to straighten my back as if I'm doing a yogic relaxation. The playful allegro thrills me, lifting my spirits, but the wistful adagio provokes sad emotions and tears. I open my eyes and gaze into the gloom. Due to lack of sleep, I start hallucinating and hearing voices over the music whispering threats. I'm at breaking point. Although I have accepted that I committed crimes and deserve to be punished, no one should have to live like this. I'm furious at myself for making the series of reckless decisions that put me in here and for losing absolutely everything. As violins crescendo in my ears, I remember what my life used to be like.

OTHER BOOKS BY SHAUN ATTWOOD

War on Drugs Series Book 1
Pablo Escobar: Beyond Narcos

The mind-blowing true story of Pablo Escobar and the Medellín Cartel beyond their portrayal on Netflix.

Colombian drug lord Pablo Escobar was a devoted family man and a psychopathic killer; a terrible enemy, yet a wonderful friend. While donating millions to the poor, he bombed and tortured his enemies – some had their eyeballs removed with hot spoons. Through ruthless cunning and America's insatiable appetite for cocaine, he became a multi-billionaire, who lived in a $100-million house with its own zoo.

Pablo Escobar: Beyond Narcos demolishes the standard good versus evil telling of his story. The authorities were not hunting Pablo down to stop his cocaine business. They were taking over it.

War on Drugs Series Book 2
American Made: Who Killed Barry Seal?
Pablo Escobar or George HW Bush

Set in a world where crime and government coexist, *American Made* is the jaw-dropping true story of CIA pilot Barry Seal that the Hollywood movie starring Tom Cruise is afraid to tell.

Barry Seal flew cocaine and weapons worth billions of dollars into and out of America in the 1980s. After he became a government informant, Pablo Escobar's Medellin Cartel offered a million for him alive and half a million dead. But his real trouble began after he threatened to expose the dirty dealings of George HW Bush.

American Made rips the roof off Bush and Clinton's complicity in cocaine trafficking in Mena, Arkansas.

"A conspiracy of the grandest magnitude." Congressman Bill Alexander on the Mena affair.

War on Drugs Series Book 3
We Are Being Lied To: The War on Drugs

A collection of harrowing, action-packed and interlinked true stories that demonstrate the devastating consequences of drug prohibition.

Party Time

In *Party Time*, Shaun Attwood arrives in Phoenix, Arizona a penniless business graduate from a small industrial town in England. Within a decade, he becomes a stock-market millionaire.

But he is leading a double life.

After taking his first Ecstasy pill at a rave in Manchester as a shy student, Shaun becomes intoxicated by the party lifestyle that changes his fortune. Making it his personal mission to bring the English rave scene to the Arizona desert, Shaun becomes submerged in a criminal underworld, throwing parties for thousands of ravers and running an Ecstasy ring in competition with the Mafia mass murderer "Sammy The Bull" Gravano.

As greed and excess tear through his life, Shaun experiences eye-watering encounters with Mafia hit men and crystal-meth addicts, extravagant debaucheries with superstar DJs and glitter girls, and ingests enough drugs to kill a herd of elephants. This is his story.

Hard Time New Edition

"Makes the Shawshank Redemption look like a holiday camp" – NOTW

After a SWAT team smashed down stock-market millionaire Shaun Attwood's door, he found himself inside of Arizona's deadliest jail and locked into a brutal struggle for survival.

Shaun's hope of living the American Dream turned into a nightmare of violence and chaos, when he had a run-in with Sammy the Bull Gravano, an Italian Mafia mass murderer.

In jail, Shaun was forced to endure cockroaches crawling in his ears at night, dead rats in the food and the sound of skulls getting cracked against toilets. He meticulously documented the conditions and smuggled out his message.

Join Shaun on a harrowing voyage into the darkest recesses of human existence.

HARD TIME provides a revealing glimpse into the tragedy, brutality, dark comedy and eccentricity of prison life.

Featured worldwide on Nat Geo Channel's Locked-Up/Banged-Up Abroad Raving Arizona.

Prison Time

Sentenced to 9½ years in Arizona's state prison for distributing Ecstasy, Shaun finds himself living among gang members, sexual predators and drug-crazed psychopaths. After being attacked by a Californian biker in for stabbing a girlfriend, Shaun writes about the prisoners who befriend, protect and inspire him. They include T-Bone, a massive African American ex-Marine who risks his life saving vulnerable inmates from rape, and Two Tonys, an old-school Mafia murderer who left the corpses of his rivals from Arizona to Alaska. They teach Shaun how to turn incarceration to his advantage, and to learn from his mistakes.

Shaun is no stranger to love and lust in the heterosexual world, but the tables are turned on him inside. Sexual advances come at him from all directions, some cleverly disguised, others more sinister – making Shaun question his sexual identity.

Resigned to living alongside violent, mentally-ill and drug-addicted inmates, Shaun immerses himself in psychology and philosophy to try to make sense of his past behaviour, and begins applying what he learns as he adapts to prison life. Encouraged by Two Tonys to explore fiction as well, Shaun reads over 1000 books which, with support from a brilliant psychotherapist, Dr Owen, speed along his personal development. As his ability to deflect daily threats improves, Shaun begins to look forward to his release with optimism and a new love waiting for him. Yet the words of Aristotle from one of Shaun's books will prove prophetic: "We cannot learn without pain."

ABOUT SHAUN ATTWOOD

Shaun Attwood is a former stock-market millionaire and Ecstasy supplier turned public speaker, author and activist, who is banned from America for life. His story was featured worldwide on National Geographic Channel as an episode of Locked Up/Banged Up Abroad called Raving Arizona (available on YouTube).

Shaun's writing – smuggled out of the jail with the highest death rate in America run by Sheriff Joe Arpaio – attracted international media attention to the human rights violations: murders by guards and gang members, dead rats in the food, cockroach infestations…

While incarcerated, Shaun was forced to reappraise his life. He read over 1,000 books in just under six years. By studying original texts in psychology and philosophy, he sought to better understand himself and his past behaviour. He credits books as being the lifeblood of his rehabilitation.

Shaun tells his story to schools to dissuade young people from drugs and crime. He campaigns against injustice via his books and blog, Jon's Jail Journal. He has appeared on the BBC, Sky News and TV worldwide to talk about issues affecting prisoners' rights.

As a best-selling true-crime author, Shaun is presently writing a series of action-packed books exposing the War on Drugs, which feature Pablo Escobar and the Cali Cartel.

CPSIA information can be obtained
at www.ICGtesting.com
Printed in the USA
BVHW072259291020
592123BV00014B/2191